D1389549

= **LETTS** =

*Contemporary Crafts*

# Basket Making

## OLIVIA ELTON BARRATT

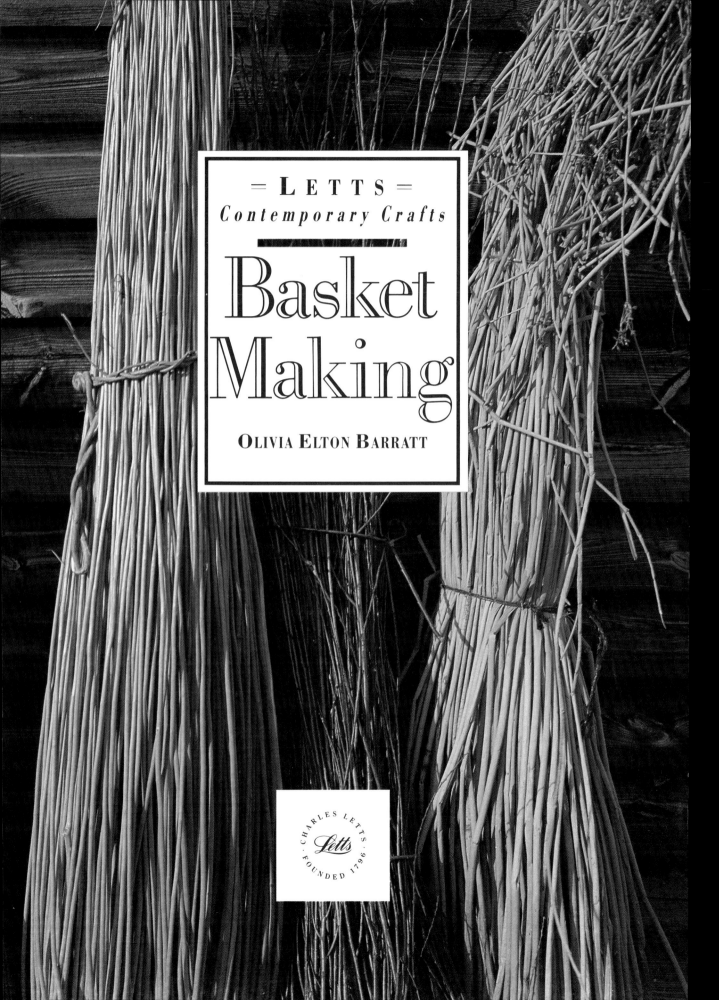

= LETTS =
*Contemporary Crafts*

# Basket Making

OLIVIA ELTON BARRATT

CHARLES LETTS · *Letts* · FOUNDED 1796

*DEDICATION*

*For Rebecca Golding Singer*

ACKNOWLEDGEMENTS

*The author thanks Mary Butcher, Kay Johnson and Vivienne Jones for checking the manuscript, and the contributors for their skill, hard work and enthusiasm.*

Designed and edited by
Anness Law Limited
4a The Old Forge
7 Caledonian Road
London N1 9DX

First published 1990
by Charles Letts & Co Ltd
Diary House, Borough Road
London SE1 1DW

© 1990 Charles Letts & Co Ltd

All our Rights Reserved. No part of this publication may be reproduced, stored in a retrieval system, or transmitted, in any form or by any means, electronic, mechanical, photocopying, recording or otherwise, without the prior permission of Charles Letts Publishers.

ISBN 1 85238 109 4

A CIP catalogue record for this book is available from the British Library.

"Letts" is a registered trademark of Charles Letts (Scotland) Ltd.

Project Editor: Sue Egerton-Jones
Creative Director: Peter Bridgewater
Photographer: Zul Mukhida
Illustrator: Lorraine Harrison

Printed and bound in Portugal by
Printer Portugesa

# CONTENTS

INTRODUCTION                                      6

MATERIALS AND EQUIPMENT                           8

BASIC TECHNIQUES                                 14

GALLERY                                          27

**PROJECTS**

EGG BASKET IN HEDGEROW MATERIALS                 35

HEDGEROW TRAY                                    41

SPIRALLING CANE BOWL                             47

RUSH BOATER                                      53

RUSH BOX IN DIAGONAL WEAVE                       59

FRAME BASKET                                     65

BROWN AND WHITE WILLOW DOG BASKET                71

FRUIT BASKET IN UNSTRIPPED WILLOW                77

OVAL FLOWER AND VEGETABLE BASKET                 83

WILLOW LETTER TRAY                               89

USEFUL INFORMATION                               94

INDEX                                            95

# INTRODUCTION

Basketmaking is one of the oldest skills in the world, pre-dating pottery and weaving. As soon as people became aware of the need for a container, they would have used whatever natural materials were available, twisting and weaving them into some sort of basket. The materials to hand, whether willows, rushes, straw, roots, or even trees and their bark, would have been dictated by the climate. Basketmakers would have developed the techniques to work them into useful objects and we can see evidence of their skill today. The remnants of coiled work dated at about 10,000 BC have been found in the Middle East, and in Africa fragments of pot have been found with the imprint of basket work on them, dating back beyond 8,000 BC. The Dead Sea Scrolls, dated around 200 BC, were found in plaited baskets.

The material available would have influenced the way in which it was used, and so basketmaking techniques developed independently in different continents. Coiled or plaited and stitched baskets like the early Middle Eastern examples would make use of fine grasses and roots, or straw and rushes. Stake and strand weaving methods like those in our everyday shopping baskets would be used for strong material like willow or rattan cane. Flat leaves would be used for woven mats and baskets, which could also be made in such materials as birch bark. The methods used in the early centuries are still in use, and a basketmaker today could make a willow chair exactly like one illustrated in a carving of a Roman interior.

Differences in culture and environment led to very different styles in design and embellishment, and it was not until travel between continents became easier that countries began to export their own traditions in basketmaking, and to absorb those of others. The large numbers of immigrants from many different countries to North America during the last 200 years, for instance, means that they are particularly rich in styles and techniques. The immigrants passed on their own skills as well as absorbing those of their new neighbours, and adapted their own techniques to the materials available in the new country.

Baskets were central to every stage of life, and not just for carrying things. Houses were built of basketwork, then packed and daubed with mud to make them weather-proof; babies were rocked in basket cradles, their parents sat in basket chairs and were buried in basket coffins. Goods were carried in baskets, crops harvested into baskets, carriages were constructed out of basketwork, and warriors went to war with basket shields. As industry developed, baskets were used in mines, mills, weaving sheds, and many other working situations. Even into the twentieth century the basket retained its importance.

The development of plastics, lightweight metals, and pressed cardboard gave rise in the mid-twentieth century to cheap disposable containers for goods. The delivery boy and his basket gave way to the wire supermarket trolley. The commercial market for baskets declined, and with it the number of basketmakers dwindled, the skills being kept alive mainly by elderly craftsmen and enthusiasts.

The respect in which the basketmaker was held dwindled too. In many countries where baskets took their place in rituals and beliefs, the status of the maker had been high. Superb baskets have come down to us from the American Indians, where the standard of the basketmaker (often a woman) reflected her status in the tribe, and on her death her best work might be burned, or buried with her. By the mid-twentieth century, in Britain at least, the basketmaker was often regarded as an archaic figure, or even as a joke.

Towards the end of this century the pendulum is swinging the other way again, assisted by an increasing interest in and concern for our environment. A container made of environmentally sustainable materials makes sense, whether it be willow, rush, bamboo, coiled roots, or re-cycled cardboard collected from urban rubbish skips. Suddenly everyone wants to use baskets again. Look through the pages of any magazine aimed at fashion, the home, or the environment generally, and you find that baskets are featured everywhere, both as functional and as decorative objects. From the little miracles of split bamboo from China, or the beautiful traditional shapes of English willow log baskets or hampers, to the superb simplicity of Shaker splint baskets, we can see and enjoy examples from every country in the world, in a wonderful range of materials. Just look around you the next time you have lunch in a restaurant, visit a department store, or go to a craft fair. You will be amazed at the number of baskets you will see in use, let alone those offered for sale. The craft is taking on a new lease of life, and basketmakers are hard put to keep up with demand.

The increasing use of baskets has brought with it a growing interest in basketmaking, both as a way of life and as a leisure activity. The old-established firms who hung on through the lean times are taking on new employees, and the demand for the whole range of their products – from shopping to balloon baskets – has meant both the continuance of traditional designs and the development of new ones. Many people who learned the skills for pleasure are turning them to good use, and finding great fascination in learning techniques from many different countries. There are flourishing associations of basketmakers, who are encouraging the sharing of information with the teaching of basketmaking at summer schools and leisure classes, and by developing contacts between basketmakers of different countries. Everywhere there is an increased need for information, instruction, and inspiration.

This book addresses these needs. The basketmakers whose work is illustrated in the Gallery demonstrate many different aspects of their craft that are attracting interest today. Their work ranges from traditional, functional designs which are beautiful because of their integrity and appropriateness to their purpose, through a variety of exciting materials and styles, to the sort of individual, decorative piece to be found in a gallery or exhibition. In the Projects section, the materials they have used, and the way to prepare them, are concisely described, together with the necessary tools and equipment and their uses.

The Materials and Techniques section covers the basic skills needed to make some simple baskets, and is illustrated with photographs to take the reader through the different stages. These basic techniques will help you to try out the baskets from the Projects for yourself. The projects have been specially designed by a selection of basketmakers to illustrate their own particular styles. The clear instructions and step-by-step photographs will encourage progression from the simplest project to the more complex. The projects use basic techniques together with new ones relating to each particular basket, and encourage readers to experiment, and develop further along their own lines.

You will find, therefore, that many of the projects are adaptable. You may feel that a basket made in the biggest willow, which would be thick and heavy to handle, does not quite suit your circumstances. Make it up in willow which is a couple of sizes smaller instead. You can use the same instructions, and the result will be a considerably smaller basket. Several of the projects have been designed to use one size of willow only, which simplifies the buying of materials. If you have no opportunity to go out and gather your own material for the 'hedgerow' baskets, use unstripped brown willow, which gives a lovely natural look. Centre cane is quick to prepare and convenient for those who can only snatch odd moments for basketmaking, and less bulky than willow if you have little storage space. There are ways round all the problems, and none of them will keep you from making baskets.

This is intended to be an inspirational book. It shows you what can be achieved by basketmakers of skill and distinction, and encourages you to start out along the road they have travelled. The instruction in it is simple and basic, and there are many techniques that it does not cover. It takes much practice and considerable study to become an accomplished basketmaker; there are specialist books to help the serious student. I hope this book will help you to find pleasure and satisfaction in creating baskets, and inspire you to continue the journey.

# MATERIALS AND EQUIPMENT

If you study the baskets in the Gallery closely, you will appreciate the wide range of materials used. Some of them are grown and harvested specifically for the purpose and sold commercially, some is 'hedgerow' material, gathered quite literally from hedges, woods, gardens and ponds, and some is manufactured, such as cardboard, plastic and wire.

### WILLOW

These are all the *Salix* species. They grow in many countries of the world, and for centuries have been a cultivated crop for basketmaking. *S. triandra* is the one generally grown, but other varieties such as *S. viminalis* and *S. Purpurea* are also used, and a great variety of different coloured barks can be found.

Cultivated willow is planted in regularly spaced rows, and cut right back to the stool (the short length of stem above the ground) every year. First year growth is used for baskets, though some are grown on for another season to provide thicker sticks for furniture making. A good willow bed can last for 40 years or more.

Harvesting is done in the winter when the sap is down. The willow is sorted, and prepared for sale in three different ways:

● *Unstripped,* known as green when fresh, and brown when dried, is traditionally used for agricultural baskets, and is very popular today.

● *Buff,* which has been boiled to drive the tannin from the bark into the willow, and then stripped to give a lovely chestnut colour, is used for the majority of shopping and working baskets.

● *White,* which is obtained by standing the bundles in pits of water until the spring, and stripping when the leaves begin to sprout. This leaves beautiful ivory rods, traditionally used for food or laundry baskets.

Stripping is mostly done by machine now, but it used to be done by hand and was very much a communal activity, even the children staying away from school to help.

Much of Britain's willow comes from the county of Somerset, a recognized centre of the industry, but suppliers are again appearing in other willow-growing areas. An increasing number of basketmakers plant their own small 'holt' in back yard, garden, or allotment, as they used to in the past.

Before the Second World War the Argentine was a major supplier of superb quality willow, the climate encouraging very long rods with little pith. It is now being grown commercially in Chile. Willow needs a temperate climate, with enough sun to encourage growth but not so hot that it becomes thin and brittle. In North America there has been difficulty in producing enough good quality willow, imports from Europe making up the deficiency. Now there is a network of enthusiasts experimenting with different varieties and methods, and exchanging information.

Willow is sold in bundles known as 'bolts', direct from the grower, from wholesalers, or in craft shops where it is often sold in smaller quantities by weight. British suppliers export willow to a number of countries, to individuals, retailers and manufacturers.

The rods are bundled into bolts of different lengths, and the longer the rod, the thicker it is. The bolts are

traditionally measured in feet, and range from 3ft (92cm) up to 8ft (2.4m) or even bigger.

Basketmakers use different sizes of willow for different parts of a basket, and a selection of 3ft (92cm), 4ft (1.2m), and 5ft (1.5m) would be useful to the beginner. However, the contents of a bolt vary considerably in thickness, and it is possible to make up a basket from one size of bolt only (see page 15).

Willow keeps well over a period of years if kept in an airy store, preferably dark to preserve the colour.

## PREPARATION

Willow needs to be soaked in water and mellowed by leaving it wrapped in a thick, damp cloth, before it is pliable enough to use.

A tin bath or cattle trough from a junk yard or builders' supplier makes a good soaking tank, long enough to submerge all but the longest rods, which could be bent round at the tips. Weight the rods down to keep them under water. If necessary use a domestic bath. For long material, soak the tips first and wrap them while the butts are soaking.

### SOAKING TIMES

| Length | Buff/White | Brown |
|---|---|---|
| 3ft (92cm) | ¾–1 hr | 2 days |
| 4ft (1.2m) | 1–1½ hrs | 3 days |
| 5ft (1.5m) | 1½–2 hrs | 4 days |
| 6ft (1.8m) | 2–3 hrs | 5 days |
| Larger | 3–4 hrs | Up to a week |

*In an emergency, soaking in warm water will hurry things up, and brown willow reacts quite well to a really hot bath.*

### MELLOWING TIMES
● Buff and white: 4–5 hrs, or overnight
● Brown: overnight at the very least, with several days for the biggest stuff
Do not leave buff or white wrapped for more than two days, wash them off and dry out for re-use or they will go greasy and mouldy. Brown will keep wrapped for much longer.

### CENTRE CANE
Centre cane, pulp cane, rattan or reed (the name you give it depends on where you live), is a product of the Rattan plant. This is a spiny, climbing plant belonging to a subfamily of the palms called the *Calmoideae,* of which there are a number of varieties.

They grow in countries from West Africa, India, China, to the Malay Peninsula, Australia and Fiji. In South and South East Asia they are the most important commercial products of the tropical forests, providing employment for many thousands of people in their harvesting and preparation.

Harvesting is generally done by hand, but the processing is done by machine. When the cut canes are dried, the barbed outer skins are stripped off. The shiny inner casing is split into fine strips of different widths for chair cane, and coarser stuff for furniture making. The centre, or pulp cane is extruded through machines to make round and flat canes of varying thicknesses for basket and furniture making.

Cane is sold by weight, from wholesalers, craft shops, and from mail order suppliers. It is available in a range of thicknesses from fine at 1.15mm (English 00, American 1) to handle cane at 8mm (English 20, American 10) with about 18 sizes in between. Larger and smaller sizes can be found. (See page 94 for chart.) It is possible to make baskets with only a few sizes.

Remember that cane sizes vary from one supplier to another and that there will be a natural variation in the bundles. Flat band, a ribbon-like cane milled on both sides, can be obtained in about 8 sizes from 8mm to 25mm, but only the two smallest are currently available in Britain. Half round cane is available in North America in sizes comparable to centre cane, but in Britain only in 5mm.

It can be bought as natural or bleached; the bleached is whiter, softer and less resilient than the natural cane. Both kinds soak up dyes extremely well. Smoked cane is sometimes available, and this is a good brown colour.

Store cane in long straight bundles rather than tight coils, as this makes it easier to use. Cane will keep over a period of years, but it darkens and hardens with time.

### PREPARATION
Cane is very easy to prepare, the smaller sizes requiring only one or two minutes in water, with no mellowing needed. 3–4mm cane needs about five to ten minutes, often less. 5mm or thicker needs about 20 minutes if it has to be bent at a sharp angle.

Hot water speeds up the process, which should be as short as possible. Too much soaking discolours and spoils the cane.

## RUSH

*Scirpus lacustris,* the bulrush, has been used for centuries for mats, mattresses, baskets and for seating chairs, and is still widely used today. Rush carpets and log baskets are currently very popular, and woven rush hats particularly so. In Britain they are much worn by teams of Morris dancers, who choose many different styles. Rush baskets are still made commercially, although they are not as widely available as willow or cane.

The bulrush grows all over the world, but it seems that it is harvested commercially mainly in Britain and in Europe. The material varies in colour, texture and length over quite small geographical areas, and has been known to reach over 4m (13ft) in some places. It grows in deep or shallow water, in rivers, streams and ponds. Saltwater rushes tend to be harder in texture than freshwater ones.

Harvesting is done in the summer months when the sap is still high. If it is done after the sap begins to fall, the plants will have little strength in them when dried.

The rushes are cut as near to the roots as possible, and tied into bundles for drying. The air must get to the bundles to dry out the sap completely, and this can take a week or two. If the rushes were to be stored before they were quite dry, they would quickly go mouldy and would then be useless.

Rushes keep well over a period of years if stored in a dry place, and in the dark to preserve the colour.

Rushes can be bought direct from the growers, from wholesalers, craft shops and mail order suppliers. They are traditionally sold by the bolt, or bundle, but are increasingly sold by weight.

### PREPARATION

Prepare rushes by damping, not by soaking. Lay the rushes on the ground and water them with hosepipe or watering can, turning them to damp both sides.

They can be prepared in the bath, but leave the plug out and use a shower spray. Never leave the rushes in water. Soaked rushes become waterlogged and difficult to use, and shrink greatly as they dry out, producing loosely woven baskets or chairs.

Mellow them by wrapping in a thick damp cloth for about three hours. They will keep for about two days in the damp cloth before going mouldy. Do not damp more than you can use at a time.

## HEDGEROW MATERIALS

Hedgerow 'wood' are materials which can be gathered from woods, hedgerows, gardens, ponds and streams. Providing that this source of material is treated with respect, it is a wonderful way to introduce the colours, scents and textures of the countryside into your baskets. Plants from which you have taken wood should always be left in a well-pruned condition, and the plants in your own garden are the only ones you can use without permission.

Walk around your home area in summer, looking for vigorously growing one-year shoots from suitable plants. Talk to farmers, gardeners landowners and park keepers. Ask if you can have their prunings when the sap is down. They may help you to identify the plants and tell you where others may be found. Every area has a different landscape and soil; your 'woods' are local, personal, and individual, and a most enjoyable (and time-consuming) part of your basketmaking is in the finding and gathering of 'woods'.

Cut them in winter and early spring when the sap is down. The stem colours often improve after frosts. The qualities to look for are:
- Materials supple enough to bend round your hand without cracking
- First year growth (second year is too woody), or suckers, from hedges, trees and shrubs
- Exciting colours
- Scent
- A bloom on the stems
- Cones, catkins, attractive bark or buds to add interest
- Straight twigs of reasonable length, with a gentle taper from butt to tip
- Long trailing pieces of climbing plants for weaving
- Thick woods for handle bows

Look for materials for each part of the basket, sets of 24 to 30 rods, long, supple and strong enough for stakes, finer stuff for weaving.

Plants vary in the way they grow in different parts of the world, and with the seasons, and will react differently when used, so it is only possible to give general guidelines.

For general use in all parts of the basket, particularly for stakes, willows are the most useful, *S. alba* providing green, yellow, orange and red coloured bark, and

*S. daphnoides* a purplish bark which develops a blue bloom. *Cornus alba* (dogwood) red and green, and *Viburnum cassinoides* (witherod) are good for all purposes.

For weavers, which do not have to bend so sharply, there are many possibilities. Trees and shrubs such as *Latrix sp.* (larch), *Tilia sp.* (lime). *Populus sp.* and *Populus gileadensis* (poplar and balsam poplar), *Ulmus sp.* (elm), and *Symphoricarpus albus* (snowberry) are a few suggestions.

Long trailing plants include *Clematis sp.* (clematis and wild clematis, used peeled), *Vinca sp.* (periwinkle). *Lonicera sp.* (honeysuckle, used peeled or unpeeled), *Rosa canina* (dog rose, stripped of its thorns by pulling through a thick cloth), or bramble, similarly stripped.

Handle bows can be cut from *Corylus sp.* (hazel) and *Fraxinus sp.* (ash).

Soft materials can also be used and anything with long, strap-like leaves can be cut in the summer when the sap is high, dried, and re-damped for use as weavers, or for plaiting. Plants such as *Typha lattifolia* (reedmace or cattails), *Narcissus sp.* and *Iridaceae* (wild and cultivated iris) are all useful.

### PREPARATION

Tie your material in bundles and label it, then leave it in a sheltered spot to dry out until it reaches the stage known as 'clung', when it will be supple enough to work with but will not shrink too much later on. This may take two or three weeks, depending on the woods, but elm and bramble can be used immediately, and so can dogwood in an emergency.

Use your material before it dries right out in late spring – it will be no use when it is completely dry. Hedgerow woods are generally used without soaking; only the willows can be successfully soaked as a rule.

### MODERN MATERIALS

Many contemporary basketmakers are producing exciting work using such materials as: cardboard, cut into strips, painted and varnished; plastic packing tape, either scavenged or bought; wires and plastic-coated wire; nettings; plastics in sheet form, and cut-up plastic bottles; newsprint; film strip; yarns and fabrics.

The baskets can be practical as well as exciting. Well-varnished cardboard wears almost like leather, plastics are indestructible (although they will crack), and yarns have many uses, particularly in coil work.

### DYEING

Cane and willow can both be dyed satisfactorily, creating a whole range of colour possibilities.

If you prefer to work with natural dyes, there is a great deal of information now available. However, there are excellent commercial dyes which are comparatively simple to use, with a good choice of shades.

You can obtain good results using dyes sold in small containers for home use. The best ones are those for use on vegetable fibres. Some of these are cold water dyes, some require boiling up, but this is not difficult.

Dyes are poisonous, so any pans, spoons and tongs must be kept exclusively for the purpose. Wear rubber gloves and a plastic apron, and a mask as well if you plan to do a great deal of dyeing at once and keep the room ventilated.

Follow the directions on the packet for quantities and mixing. Some dyes only require a tablespoon of salt and a kettle of boiling water per container, and mix very easily.

Use an old saucepan if you are going to boil the material in the dye. A plastic bowl or bucket will do if you are not going to boil. Add enough hot water to cover the material.

Coil cane into manageable quantities, and put it dry into the dye bath. Keep turning it until the required colour is reached. You can rinse the cane in cold water, or drain it thoroughly and use it straight away. It does not seem to bleed too much into other colours.

Buff, white and brown willow all take dyes to varying degrees, with beautiful results, but the length of the willow makes it difficult to handle in a domestic situation. Small quantities of fine rods, however, can be pre-soaked and tied into coils before dyeing in bowl or bucket.

For small quantities of longer lengths, you can use a plastic drainpipe with a permanent seal at one end and a screw top at the other. This ensures that the full length of the willow can be submerged. It can be rolled on the ground if necessary. Do this outside, with a suitable drain available so that the dye can be disposed of.

**SKEINING TOOLS**
*A cleave, a tool with fins to split the willow into skeins.*
*A shave, like a miniature plane, to strip off the pith.*
*An upright, like a vetical plane with two blades shave the skein to an even thickness.*

**HOOP**
*Cane or willow hoops in various sizes for holding the stakes upright. (You can tie the stakes together with string instead.)*

**GREASE HORN**
*Container full of tallow for greasing the bodkin. The bodkin can be rubbed with soap instead.*

**WEIGHTS**
*Metal weights or heavy stones, about 1½ kg (3 lb) to hold the basket steady.*

**SHEARS**
*Pointed ones, for cutting thick rods and trimming.*

**ROUND-NOSED PLIERS**
*For centre cane, to squeeze the cane before bending sharply, to prevent cracking.*

**SCISSORS**
*With sharp points, for trimming rushes.*

**RAPPING IRON**
*Heavy metal tool like a big file, but smooth, used narrow edge downwards for compressing the weave. The ring at the end can be used as a Commander, to straighten willow rods. (A heavy file, taped round to protect the willow, would substitute.)*

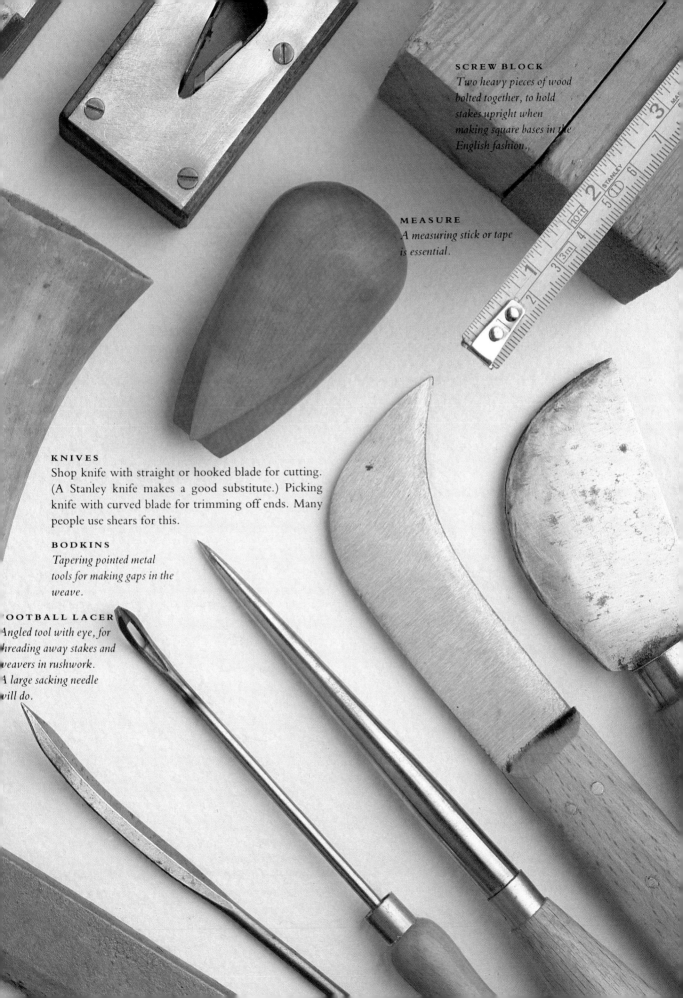

**SCREW BLOCK**
*Two heavy pieces of wood bolted together, to hold stakes upright when making square bases in the English fashion.*

**MEASURE**
*A measuring stick or tape is essential.*

**KNIVES**
Shop knife with straight or hooked blade for cutting. (A Stanley knife makes a good substitute.) Picking knife with curved blade for trimming off ends. Many people use shears for this.

**BODKINS**
*Tapering pointed metal tools for making gaps in the weave.*

**OOTBALL LACER**
*Angled tool with eye, for hreading away stakes and veavers in rushwork. A large sacking needle vill do.*

# BASIC TECHNIQUES

**GETTING STARTED**

There must be nearly as many different ways of making baskets as there are basketmakers, but there are techniques which are common to most cultures and most materials.

This section will take you through the basic essentials, enabling you to approach the projects later in the book with some confidence. It will show you how some basketmaking techniques are used with different materials, and how they can be varied to achieve different shapes and styles. It will not cover every technique, or show you how to make every kind of basket, but there are many specialist books available to the serious student of basketmaking. The special features that individual basketmakers have given to their designs in this book are explained in the relevant projects.

**GLOSSARY OF TERMS**

This list of technical terms, with explanations, will help you to follow the instructions.

**back** The outside of the curve on a willow rod.

**base** Basket bottom.

**belly** The inside of the curve on a willow rod.

**butt** Thick end of a willow rod.

**by-stakes** Used in canework, inserted into the upsett beside each stake to add strength.

**changing the stroke** Process in canework for achieving even transition between rows.

**checkweave** Rush weave with single weaver in 'over one, under one' sequence.

**coil basket** Basket made from a core, coiled and stitched together.

**cram** Sharpened stake turned down into the weave.

**crown** Reversed saucer shape given to basket bases.

**cutting out** Selecting appropriate material.

**diagonal weave** 'Over one, under one' weave on the diagonal.

**elbow** Point where a stake is bent down for a border.

**English rand** Willow weave using one rod at a time.

**fitching** Reverse pairing used above open sections.

**flow** Outward or inward curve of a basket.

**foot track** Round of weaving for basket to stand on.

**frame basket** Basket worked over a frame or hoop.

**French rand** Willow weave using one weaver per stake.

**handle bow** Thick rod which forms basket handle.

**handle liners** Temporary markers for handle bow.

**hoop** Willow ring to hold stakes upright, or to form frame of basket.

**notch** Gap in weave to form an opening.

**packing** Extra weaving to alter the level.

**pairing** Weave using two rods crossing each other between stakes.

**pegging** Method of securing a basket handle.

**picking off** Trimming off ends of material.

**pricking up or down** Pricking the rod with a knife to bend it sharply without cracking.

**rand** Weave with one weaver in 'over one, under one' sequence.

**reverse pairing** Weave sloping the opposite way to pairing.

**reverse waling** Weave sloping the opposite way to waling.

**rod border** Method of weaving away stakes for a border.

**rods** Sticks of willow.

**roped handle** Handle made from a bow wrapped with finer rods.

**scallom** Long slanting cut on the butt of a stake for fastening to the base.

**siding** The weaving on the side of a basket.

**skeins** Willow rods split and scraped to make fine flat strips.

**slath** Centre of base where the bottom sticks cross each other.

**slath rods** Rods used in an underfoot oval base.

**slewing** Randing weave using several weavers at once.

**slype** Slanting cut on the butt of a rod for easy insertion into the weave.

**split slath** French method of forming a slath by splitting the sticks.

**square work** Square or rectangular baskets.

**stake** Upright rods in the sides of a stake and strand basket.

**stake and strand basket** Basket with weaving over a skeleton of rods.

**staking up** Inserting side stakes in a stake and strand basket, and pricking them up.

**stroke** Single movement of a weave or border, like a stitch in sewing.

**stuff** Name given to materials by basketmakers.

**tip** Thin end of a willow rod.

**trac border** Method of turning down stakes for a border.

**twill weave** Randing over groups of stakes in progressive pattern.

**underfoot slath** English method of forming a slath without splitting the sticks, holding the work down with the feet.

**upsett** Pricking up the stakes and weaving the lower rows of a basket.

**waling** Strong weave using three weavers crossing between stakes.

**weaver** Length of material for weaving.

### THE PARTS OF THE BASKET

The *base* is made separately, in a round, oval, or angular shape, with bottom sticks to form a framework for weaving. It is domed, or *crowned* upwards, to strengthen the point where the side stakes are driven into it and pricked up to form the sides.

The exception here is rush, where the stakes run right through the basket from border to border, and the basket is made on a rigid mould to hold the shape.

The *siding* is worked in a choice of weaves, and a band of waling is put on at the top for strength.

The *border* is formed by bending down and interweaving the stakes.

Handles, lids, fastenings and partitions can be added.

### HANDLING THE MATERIALS

Natural materials all have their different characteristics, and you will make better baskets if you become familiar with them.

Treat willow firmly but gently; where it kinks, there it will stay, and you will not be able to smooth the kink out, so try to get your strokes right first time.

Hedgerow materials can be difficult and erratic to handle, but the charm of their appearance, feel, and scent more than makes up for this. Do not make things difficult for yourself by using material too thick or too thin for what you want to make. Choose simple styles.

Cane is versatile, ready for use very quickly, and is comparatively easy to handle.

Rushes are much stronger than you might think. Weave tightly for firm baskets, but pull steadily rather than sharply, to avoid breakages.

### SELECTING MATERIAL

Careful selection of the material, or *cutting out the stuff,* as it is sometimes called, is the first essential process in achieving a well-made basket.

Size and proportion in the different parts of the basket are very important. This is a useful guide:

- Bottom sticks, thickest stuff
- Side stakes, next thickest
- Walers, medium
- Weavers, thinnest

Sometimes the base is woven with the finest weavers, sometimes with quite thick rods, depending on the type of basket.

Good results can be obtained either by selecting material from bolts of several different sizes, or by dividing a single bolt carefully into thick, medium and thin. Several of the projects in this book have been worked with carefully graded material all from the same sized bolt.

Remember that the border of a basket is important, and the side stakes you choose must have a good proportion where they turn down for the border.

Discard blemished rods when choosing stakes. Perhaps you will be able to use them up in the base or side weaving of another basket.

Prepare your material as described on pages 9–11, and keep willow and rush wrapped in a damp cloth as you work. Be prepared to put your basket back into the water for a while during construction. If it dries out too much, the rods will crack or break and spoil your work. Many basketmakers use a bucket and sponge, or a spray bottle, to keep their work damp.

**WORKING POSITION**

Most professional basketmakers prefer to work sitting on the floor, on a plank of wood (known as 'on the plank'), or on a low stool. They work with the basket between their knees, or on a lapboard, a large piece of wood lying across the lap and sloping to the ground between the feet. The basket is held in place with a weight, or pinned to the board with a bodkin. This is a very comfortable position, and makes the basket easier to control, but you may prefer to work with it on a table, and either stand, or sit on a chair.

After staking up, work the first upsett row with the basket on its side. After that you can stand it upright, with a weight in it to hold it firm.

**BASIC TECHNIQUES**

The following examples of a shopping basket and an oval cane platter provide an explanation of the basic techniques used to create many types of basket.

**WILLOW SHOPPING BASKET**

A round shopping basket made in willow uses simple basic techniques. The pierced slath is a French technique. The basket has a base diameter of 20cm (8in), a top diameter of 40cm (16in) and is 26cm (10½in) tall at the border. You could use buff or white willow, and should prepare the material as described on page 9.

**YOU WILL NEED:**

1.5 m (5 ft) willow sorted into different thicknesses.
- 6 very thick rods for bottom sticks
- 8 medium rods for weaving the base
- 24 thick rods for side stakes
- 14 medium rods for upsett
- 48 thinnest rods for siding
- 6 medium rods for top wale
- 1 very thick rod for handle bow
- 8 thin rods for handle wrapping
- Knife, shears, bodkin, rapping iron and a weight

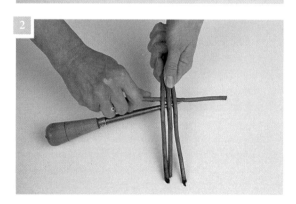

### THE BASE

To form the base, cut six bottom sticks, 25cm (10in) long, from the butts of the thickest rods 5cm (2in) longer than base diameter. With with knife or bodkin, pierce three sticks in the centre and across the natural curve (**picture 1**). Thread them on the bodkin, and thread the other three through the slits.

Alternate butts and tips throughout to distribute the thickness and use the natural curve to make a domed shape (**picture 2**). This is the *slath*.

To tie in the slath with pairing, use two medium weavers. Poke the tips down the slit to the left of one group of three sticks. Bring one weaver round the back of the group to the right, and out to the front again (**picture 3**).

To make a pairing stroke, pass the left-hand weaver over the right one, behind the next group of stakes, and out to the front again. Each weaver takes it in turn to be the left-hand weaver.

Work two complete rounds over the four groups of three sticks. Then work each stroke behind a single stick only, separating the sticks and pulling the weave in tight to the centre (**picture 4**).

Continue to weave, separating the sticks evenly, and bending them a little to form the crown.

When the butt ends of the weavers are reached, re-place them both with new butts, left-hand one first. With the old butt towards you, slide the new butt in on its right, and do the next stroke with it. Repeat with right butt (**picture 5**). Always replace both weavers at once.

When you reach the tips of the new rods, replace with new tips in the same way. Discard the very thinnest part of the tips.

When the base measures 20cm (8in) across, finish with tips. Tuck them away into the row below. (The base should be nicely crowned, and the sticks an even distance apart.)

Pick off all ends of weavers smoothly, using picking knife or shears, making sloping cuts. Pick off sticks close against the weave (**picture 6**).

### STAKING UP

Slype 24 thick rods on the belly. With the base crown downwards, drive the stakes in slype upwards, one each side of every bottom stick, as far as you can, using the bodkin to make a space.

● Turn the base over crown upwards. Push the knife point a little way into a stake close to the base and turn it about 90°, while lifting the rod up (**picture 7**). This is *pricking up*; it breaks up the fibre of the rod, and allows it to bend sharply without cracking. (The back of each rod is towards the inside of the basket, giving greater control of the flow. Staking up with belly outwards helps a barrel shape.)

Prick up all the stakes, bend them up, put on a hoop about the same diameter as finished basket or tie together with string. Put it on high up, and bend a stake round it to hold it there.

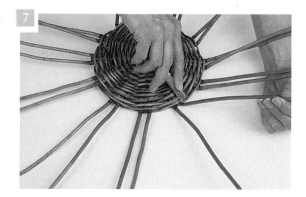

## THE UPSETT

● Lay the basket on its side, and start the upsett with a four-rod wale with medium weavers. (The basket stands on this round of waling.)

Push four tips well into the weave to the left of a stake. Take rods behind that stake, and bring out to the front again, one in each of next four spaces.

● To make a waling stroke, pass the left-hand weaver over the other three (and in front of three stakes), behind one stake, and out to the front in the next space (**picture 8**). Repeat with each weaver in turn.

Pull the stroke emerging between a left-hand stake of a pair and the bottom stick well down into the gap, to help to separate the pairs of stakes evenly.

● When you reach the starting point again, pull one weaver down between the left-hand stake and the stick. Leave it to be cut off later. Continue with three weavers, in front of two, behind one (**picture 9**).

This three-rod wale lies on the side of the basket. Stand the basket upright on table or plank, and weight it down. Continue to wale, controlling the angle of the stakes to establish the outward flow.

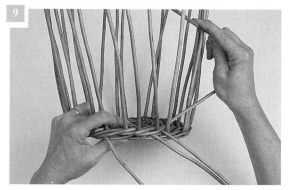

● When you reach the butts, join in three new butts, left-hand one first. To join, draw each butt in turn to the left, slide a new butt in on the right in the same space, and do a stroke with it (**picture 10**).

Work the new rods out to the tips. Waling always finishes with tips, to avoid gaps in the weave.

*Rap down* with light blows of the rapping iron between each stake to tighten up the work.

● Put in two thick rods to act as handle liners, 15cm (6in) taller than the finished basket. Slype and push them into the wale on the left of exactly opposite stakes.

● Take off the hoop. The basket should hold its shape.

THE SIDING

● Two sets of English randing, using the finest weavers. Each set has one weaver for each stake.

● To work English randing, place the butt of a rod against the inside of a stake, and weave to the right around the basket, in front of one stake and behind the next, until the weaver is resting on its own butt. Leave the surplus outside the basket. Repeat with the next rod, one place to the right (**picture 11**).

Using the shortest rods first, continue to weave in rods, one place to the right each time. Rap down the butts with the iron every three or four rods to close up the work. Use the left hand as shown, to support the stakes at the correct angle as you work. (The work builds up unevenly, but after 24 rods are worked it will be level.) Repeat with a second set of 24 rods.

● Work a top three-rod wale with medium weavers.

Put three tips into three consecutive spaces (**picture 12**). Start with tips to prevent gaps in the weave, and leave the tips outside the basket.

Wale round with these rods, joining in three more when you reach the butts. Work out to the tips (**picture 13**). This is a *set* of waling.

● Level the work with the rapping iron.

● Pick off the ends to make it easier to work the border. Trim butts on the inside where they rest against a stake. Tips of useful length can be used in a smaller basket.

THE BORDER

This will be a 'four rod behind two' border, for strength. Re-damp the basket if it has dried out, to prevent the stakes cracking as you bend them down.

● Prick down all the stakes with a knife or kink them over your thumb-nail as in the picture, or over the butt end of a thick rod, or a clothes-peg (**picture 14**).

● Starting three stakes to the left of the handle liner as shown, bring one stake down behind the two on its right, and out to the front again. Working to the right, repeat with the next three stakes.

● Take the left-hand horizontal stake (the first to be bent down), and pass it in front of two vertical stakes, behind one, and out in the next space along.

Bring the left-hand vertical behind two stakes and out in the same space, lying behind and to the right, to make a pair (**picture 15**).

Repeat these last two moves with each of the three remaining horizontal stakes, until you have four pairs.

● Using the right-hand stake of the left-hand pair each time, repeat these two moves round the basket, working around the handle liners, until two verticals remain.

● Continuing in sequence, thread the next left-hand horizontal and the left-hand vertical under the elbow of the first kinked-down stake, from inside to outside. (Try to curve rather than kink them.)

Bring last upright down behind and under the next elbow to right, and out on top of the wale.

● Lay the next left-hand horizontal along the border and kink it just short of the same elbow. Cut it off at an angle, leaving about 4cm (1½in) below the kink.

● Tuck the cut end vertically into the waling, to the left of the elbow, and tap it down with the iron. This is a *cram*. Cram the next left-hand horizontal down to the left of the next elbow.

● The next left-hand horizontal is crammed down to the left of the handle liner (**picture 16**). The picture also shows a pair of rods, with a single on its right. The right-hand stake of the pair is crammed in to the left of the next elbow beyond the handle liner, and the remaining single in the next place along. (The rods to the left of the pair have all finished their work.)

● Pick off the border closely and smoothly.

THE HANDLE
● Take out the handle liners. Then take the thickest rod you can find, slype the butt and insert it in one of the gaps, as far down the side as you can. Use the bodkin to enlarge the space if necessary.

Bring the other end of the rod over to estimate the length needed, and cut it off. An 18cm (7in) space between handle and border is enough – a long handle is a weak one. Slype and insert the cut-off end, take care not to kink it.

● Slype four fine rods, insert outside bow, in same space, getting them well down below wale.

Taking the four rods as a group, wrap them over the bow from left to right, and bring them underneath it. Repeat this twice more, finishing inside the basket on its other side. The rods must not kink or cross each other.

● Repeat with four rods from the other side (**picture 17**). These rods lie in the gaps left by the first, and should fill them. Put in an extra rod on the right of a group if they do not.

● On the outside, make a hole with the bodkin below the waling on the right of the bow. Keeping the wrapping rods in their correct order, bring them through this hole and pull them tight.

● Wrap them up to the left, behind the bow, and down again from right to left, keeping them in order (**picture 18**). You will see that a fifth rod was added to fill a space on the bow.

● Make similar gap through waling on the left of the bow, and thread tips to inside, pulling them tight.

Bring them out again in the first space, and thread back to the inside beyond the next stake on the right.

● Pick off the ends against a stake. Repeat on the other side.

### VARIATIONS OF THE SHOPPING BASKET

Hedgerow materials could be used for the shopping basket, giving it a different appearance. Alternatively you could make it in centre cane, with a few differences in technique. Prepare the cane as on page 9.

**You will need** cane in the following English sizes:
● No. 15 for bottom sticks
● No. 12 for side stakes and bye-stakes
● Nos. 10 or 8 for walers
● Nos. 8 or 6 for weavers and handle wrappers
● No. 20 for handle
● Round-nosed pliers

### TECHNIQUES FOR CANE

● To tie in the slath, use a length of No. 6 or No. 8 cane, folded in half and looped around a group of sticks. Weave the whole base in this size.

● Work three rounds of three-rod wale after the foot track, using the change of stroke as described in the Oval Platter in the next section. (Changing the stroke is not required for willow, hedgerow or rush.)

● You need to add bye-stakes for strength. Cut them a little longer than the depth of the basket. Slype and insert them into the upsett wale, one to the right of every stake and work over both together. Cut them off level with the top wale before you work the border.

● Use the change of stroke for the top wale. Thread away the border instead of cramming, as described in the Oval Platter in the next section.

● The handle could be wrapped with continuous lengths of cane, threaded under the wale and going to

and fro across the handle bow, or with separate lengths as for willow.

### OVAL CANE PLATTER

This large flat piece by Kay Johnson is designed to show the oval split slath and a variety of weaves, as well as some of the differences in technique. It is about 60 × 40cm (24 × 16in). Prepare the material by soaking the sticks in warm water for 15 minutes, and dipping the thinner cane as required.

**You will need** cane in the following English sizes:
● No. 15 natural cane      for bottom sticks
● No. 12 natural cane      for border stakes
● No. 8 natural cane      for waling
● No. 8 dyed in 3 colours for patterns
● Lapping cane dyed      for patterns
● No. 3 natural cane      for tying the slath and patterns
● No. 3 dyed      for patterns
● Shears, bodkin, and round-nosed pliers

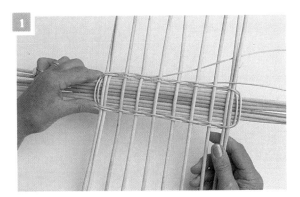

### THE SLATH

● Cut ten bottom sticks 45 cm (18 in) and six sticks 65 cm (25 in). Pierce the short sticks and thread the long sticks through. Space the short sticks to make a slath about 20cm (8in) long, with pairs at each end.

● Put two lengths of No. 8 about 22cm (9in) long down the slits on each side of the slath, to prevent it becoming 'waisted' at the sides.

● Thread a strand of No. 3 natural cane down the slit on each side, and rand them both separately round the slath for two rounds (**picture 1**). Randing is an 'over one, under one' weave.

● Add another stick about 20cm (8in) long into the weave beside the end group, to make an uneven number for later patterns.

● Use the round-nosed pliers to squeeze the end sticks close to the weave, and the outside one of each pair, ready for opening out.

● Bring the two weavers together, and pair round the end sticks and the outside ones of the pairs, to open them out. Rand down the sides to prevent the slath twisting (**picture 2**).

● Work three or four more rows, spacing the sticks evenly. Join new weavers by leaving both ends at the back. Finish the weaver ends on the back.

● For the band of coloured waling (**picture 3**), put in three dyed weavers, marking the stake immediately to the left of the left-hand weaver. Work a round of waling, finishing to the left of the marked stake.

● Now do a *change of stroke* by waling with the right-hand weaver first, then the middle one, and finally the one on the left. This makes the end of the round symmetrical.

● Work four or five rounds of waling, changing the stroke to the left of the marked stake for each round, and finishing with the ends at the back. Join by pulling the old short end to the left, and sliding the new one in on its right.

● Put in two lengths of dyed No. 8 to the right of the marked stake, and work a set of *chain pairing*. Work a round of normal pairing, changing the stroke at the end. Work a round of reverse pairing, putting the left-hand weaver under the right for each stroke (**picture 3**). Finish in sequence, threading the ends to the back.

● Cut off the weavers and work a second set, starting on the opposite side, to stagger the joins.

● Work four rounds of three-rod *slew*, using two dyed and one natural length of No. 3 cane. Slewing is randing worked with two or more canes at once. Start the ends one after the other to avoid a gap, and taper off the finish. Join with ends on the back. Do not join two weavers at once (**picture 4**).

● Use three different colours of No. 8 cane for *block waling*. You need the number of stakes to be divisible by three for this, achieved by adding the extra stake to the slath (see **picture 2**).

Starting to the right of the marked stake, work three rounds of wale, changing the stroke each time and finishing in sequence. Join where necessary as above.

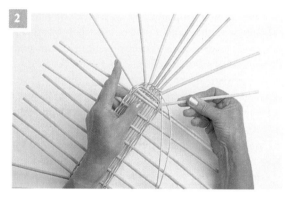

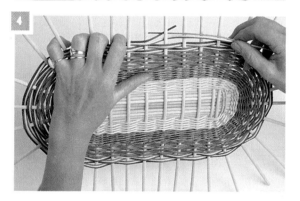

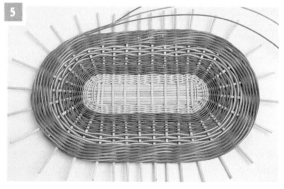

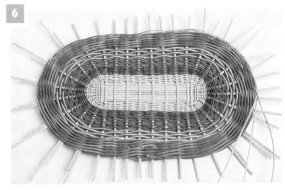

● Start a new set of waling in the same place, changing the colour positions, and work a second block of three rows (**picture 5**).

● Add extra sticks at the ends now to keep the spacing even as the work progresses.

Cut 17 sticks about 10cm (4in) long, and insert eight at one end and nine at the other. Push them down beside the existing sticks as far as the coloured waling.

● Work three rows of waling in No. 8 natural, changing the stroke and opening out the extra sticks on the first row. Space them evenly (**picture 6**).

● To work a set of *chain waling* in dyed lapping cane, work one row of waling starting to the right of the marked stake. Change the stroke, and work the second row left under right. Finish by tucking the ends through to the back in sequence.

● Starting from here, work three rounds of waling in No. 8 natural, changing the stroke each time (**picture 7**).

### THE BORDER

● Stakes have to be added to work the border, so cut 50 pieces of No. 12 natural, 40cm (15½in) long. Slype the ends. Soak them well, and mellow in a damp cloth for ten minutes for extra pliability.

● Trim off all the sticks close to the waling.

● Insert the stakes to the left of the bottom sticks, for about 6cm (2½in). Put in about ten at a time, to stop them drying out as you work (**picture 7**). Add more as the border progresses.

● Squeeze each stake to prevent cracking, about 1cm (½in) from the weave (**picture 8**).

● Work a 'three rod behind one' border. This is like the Willow Basket, but bring down only three stakes behind one to start with, and work with three pairs (**picture 9**).

● When only one stake is left upright, thread away the final stakes instead of cramming. The right-hand stake of the left-hand pair goes under the elbow of the first bent-down stake and comes out directly on top of the waling, joined by the last upright (**picture 10**).

● Thread away the last three stakes from the left-hand pairs in sequence, coming out on top of the waling. The first goes under the next elbow only; the second under an elbow and one cane; the third under an elbow and two canes (**picture 11**).

● This border has a *follow-on trac,* and you need 8–10cm (3–4in) of stake left.

Lift up three stakes, and push the left-hand one of these through to the inside under the right-hand one, on top of the wale. Move one stake to the right and repeat (**picture 12**).

Continue round the border, threading away the last two in sequence.

● Pick off all ends.

### RUSHWORK

Many of the techniques used for willow and cane are also used for rushwork; there are some vital differences. The Boater project is simple and basic, while the diagonal weave Box uses a plaiting technique.

Rush baskets require a mould; the material is too soft to retain the shape as you work. Wood and hardboard make good moulds, using tacks to hold the work in place. Tins, bowls and casseroles of the required shape and size can be used, tying the work on with string. Flower pots are good for outward flowing shapes. The mould must be at least the height of the basket.

The stakes run through from side to side. Their length needs to be: the width of the base plus twice the height of the basket, plus twice the allowance for the border. (Most borders need about 18cm (7in) at each end of the stake.)

### BASE

A small round basket starts with ten stakes interwoven at their centres into a checkweave square (over one, under one). Tie in the slath with a fine rush looped around the top left-hand stake, and pair over each stake in turn. Pull the square really tight and small, as rushes shrink, leaving gaps when dry.

Open out the second round to a circle (**picture 1**) and continue pairing until the base is the size of the block. Join in new weavers, by looping the tips around a stake and weaving the short ends away to the right.

### UPSETT AND SIDING

Secure the base to the block with tacks or string (**picture 2**). A foot track can be worked with waling or by looping the stakes one behind the other. Work the siding tightly against mould in the chosen weave, and finish with at least one round of pairing or waling.

## BORDER

*Rod* or *trac* borders can be used, and the final stages are threaded away with the lacing tool.

Dry the work on the mould, then remove and trim all the ends neatly.

## HANDLE

For a roped handle, thread an even number of rushes through the border below the pairing, butt to tip, to their halfway points.

With the border towards you, twist both groups to the right until they meet over it. Lay the right-hand group over the left one. Twist the new right-hand group once, tightly, to the right and lay it over to the left, changing hands. Repeat to make a firm twisted rope (**picture 3**).

When the handle is long enough, thread the two groups over the border and under the pairing or waling, from opposite directions, through the same space.

Thread the ends away horizontally, following the pattern of the weave, to secure and conceal them. Finish on the inside and trim when dry.

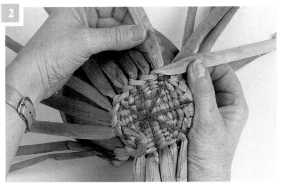

## SQUARE WORK

This is the technical term for square or rectangular baskets. The construction methods for square work vary somewhat from round or oval work, and it is generally considered more difficult.

It is not included here, but a square work Letter Tray in the French style is included in the Projects.

## COILED BASKETS

This type of basket consists of the core, and the wrapping or stitching material. The core, either a single piece or a bundle of material, is coiled around itself in a spiral, each successive coil being sewn to the previous one. It can be left exposed between stitches, or completely covered with wrapping and stitching.

Most English coiled work traditionally uses straw as an exposed core, stitched with bramble, skeined willow, chair cane or twine. This is known as lipwork.

Coiled baskets are found in many other parts of the world, using a variety of local materials and often covered by complex patterns. The shapes reflect tradition, environment, and the many uses for the baskets.

## FRAME BASKETS

These are baskets, thought to be European in origin, made by weaving over a frame or hoop which forms the rim. The frame may have a handle hoop crossing it at right angles, or handle spaces may be formed under the frame by leaving gaps in the weave. Ribs are put into the basket during weaving to give shape.

These baskets were generally made for country purposes, using whatever materials came to hand.

# GALLERY

THE BASKETMAKERS, whose work is illustrated in this section, demonstrate how exciting and varied is the range of items that can be created from different materials.

They have applied their inspiration and skills to their preferred materials, and the results are a display of baskets that reflect their own individual approach to traditional techniques and to the functional and decorative aspects that make basketmaking such an increasingly popular craft today.

~

JONI BAMFORD was originally an off-loom weaver, and her interest in American Indian culture led her to experiment with coiled work, and finally to study basketmaking in all its forms. Her aim is to make containers which unite the structural strength and diverse shapes of baskets with the rich textures and colours of woven textiles.

JOHN GALLOWAY'S
original approach to
basketmaking was traditional,
but his training in printed and
woven textiles led him to
experiment with dyed willow,
and this is now the mainstream
of his highly individual style.
The use of vibrant colours,
smooth weaves, and distinctive
shapes are the hallmarks of his
work.

· · · ·

MARY BUTCHER is primarily
interested in preserving the
traditional English willow
basketmaking techniques, but
she is also concerned with
applying them in new ways.
Her emphasis on the highest
possible standards in design and
workmanship are apparent in
her own work, and in her
policy for the Diploma Course
she runs at the London College
of Furniture.

· · · ·

A working basketmaker
apprenticed in the traditional
way, COLIN MANTHORPE
makes the full range of English
East Coast fishing, agricultural
and industrial baskets. His
baskets are characterized by an
integrity of approach and a
complete mastery of the
materials which he passes on to
the students he teaches.

· · · ·

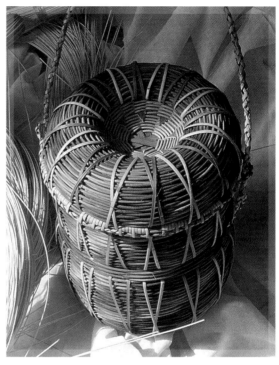

JONATHAN GORDON is completely self-taught, and he came to basketmaking by way of a love affair with country crafts. His work is characterized by extreme simplicity, and adherence to traditional design and techniques. A self-confessed romantic traditionalist in the Thomas Hardy mould, his baskets bring the past back to life and vitality.

. . . .

ALEX BURY has always found baskets irresistible, and for her the study of basketmaking was a natural development from a course of Fine Art. Some of her ideas for baskets come from experimenting with different weaves, and her travels abroad have provided inspiration for combining colour with pattern.

. . . .

OLIVIA ELTON BARRATT'S chance encounter with rush basketmaking has led to a life-long passion for this silky, supple material, full of subtle colour changes. Olivia's work demonstrates the versatility of rush as a basketmaking material, and the way in which certain weaves show off the colour and texture at their best.

. . . .

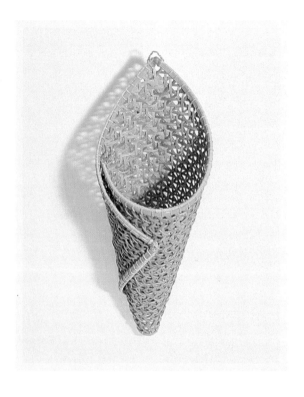

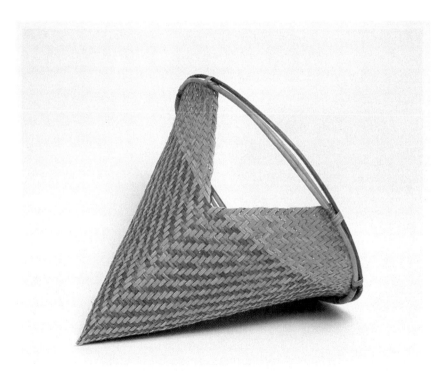

Form is the most important element in DAIL BEHENNAH'S baskets, two of which are shown here, and to her the implied function of the enclosed space is more important than their use as containers. Her sources of inspiration include ceramics, and natural forms such as rock formations, plants and seeds. The study of baskets and related forms from many cultures influences her work. *Above and below*.

· · · ·

JENNY CRISP'S approach to basketmaking is forward looking and innovative, while respecting natural materials and tradition. The traditions of English basketmaking, its qualities of purity and simplicity and the beauty of sound, functional forms have been the inspiration for her work, together with a deep love of the rural environment and things natural.

. . . .

JOHN FREITAS'S family originally came from Madeira, and he was taught by his father. He now lives and works in Somerset, a prime centre of willow culture and basketmaking in England, and his baskets show an interesting blend of English traditional ideas and his own cultural background.

. . . .

GALLERY

LEE DALBY's frame basket-making began in Brittany with gypsy friends, who split large osiers for their baskets. Welsh and Irish frame work inspired him to make superbly shaped baskets in whole willow, the traditional styles reflecting his individuality. *Top left.*

. . . .

SALLY GOYMER's view that the basketmaker's skills should be properly valued in today's world is a motivating force for achieving even higher standards. Her studies in France have given her mastery of a wide range of designs and techniques. *Top right.*

. . . .

LOIS WALPOLE has produced a positive revolution among basketmakers with her adventurous approach. Her work combines willow and cane with a glorious medley of urban gleanings. Plastic packing tape, wire, film strip and painted cardboard, combine to open up exciting new horizons. *Left.*

. . . .

Dyed cane and decorated cardboard are the main materials in POLLY POLLOCK's work. For her some of the most satisfying aspects of basket-making are colour, pattern and texture. Her baskets function as containers, a conscious design decision. *Right*.

. . . .

SHEILA WYNTER's knowledge and appreciation of plants give a special individuality to her work, which speaks strongly of her affinity with the countryside. Her hedgerow baskets complement the charm of the materials, and she makes full use of their physical and decorative attributes. *Below*.

. . . .

FRED ROGER's long experience, as apprentice, journeyman and Master Basketmaker, make him the doyen of English exponents. Now retired, his teaching and advice are sought by professional and amateur alike, and he shares his skills with generosity. *Below right*.

. . . .

# EGG BASKET IN HEDGEROW MATERIALS

SHEILA WYNTER

SIMPLE SHAPES and techniques are always the best choice for the irregular hedgerow materials.

This little basket would be useful for eggs or black-berries, and it could be made in many different combinations of material, either hedgerow or cultivated.

It uses green, red, and yellow willows for colour, with a top wale of larch, with its fascinating little cones, and one of balsam poplar for its scent.

The siding weave used is slewing, which is quick to work, and makes it possible to use a variety of different length rods.

It can be difficult to find suitable hedgerow materials for wrapping a roped handle, and here this problem is overcome by using an ash bow and pegging it just below the border. The colour and form of the ash add interest, and the pegging ensures that it stays in place.

*Base diameter: 18cm (7in); Top diameter: 28cm (11in)*
*Height at border: 18cm (7in)*

~

## MATERIALS AND EQUIPMENT

● *6 bottom sticks, pencil size, of any willow* ● *2 or 3 pieces of periwinkle, or other long thin material, to tie the slath*

The rest is a spontaneous choice of materials according to what is well clung and looking good at the time of making. In this example: red, yellow, and green willow (*S. alba*).

● *Fine rods for pairing the base* ● *23 stakes, supple and not too thick, similar to fine 1.2m (4ft) willow* ● *12 slightly thinner walers, about 38cm (15in) long* ● *24–30 supple rods for slewing* ● *A little red or Tartar dogwood (Cornus alba) for base weavers* ● *6 walers of larch (Laryx) with the cones on* ● *6 walers of balsam poplar (Populus gileadensis)* ● *An ash (Fraxinus) rod a little more than pencil thickness, about 76cm (30in)* ● *Knife* ● *Secateurs* ● *Bodkin* ● *Rapping iron* ● *Hoop*

. . . . . .

1 Make the base as described on page 17, using a length of periwinkle to tie in the slath.

Complete the base using willow and dogwood. Pick off.

Slype the 23 side stakes on the back. The curve will be towards the outside of the basket, to help achieve a good barrel shape.

Sheila's slypes show under the basket, so turn the base concave side uppermost, and drive all the side stakes well in, slype upwards, one on each side of the bottom sticks *(picture)*.

One bottom stick has only one stake, to achieve an odd number. Use the bodkin to make a space.

2 Turn the base over, prick up and upsett with yellow willow as described on page 18, but with a three-rod wale. Work a second set if needed to hold the stakes upright. Finish with tips.

The basket should flow outwards, so pull each stake outwards as you weave in front of it, and use a heavy weight to hold it in place.

A handle liner is not used.

The siding weave is slewing in red willow, which can be worked in groups of two, three or four rods. Two is just right for this one.

Lay a butt inside a stake, and work the rest of the weaver in and out of the stakes to the right, to half its length.

Lay in another butt above this rod and work the two together till the bottom one reaches its tip *(picture)*.

3 When you reach the tip of the bottom rod, lay in a new butt end above the other two rods. Continue weaving, leaving the old tip on the outside *(picture)*.

Join in new weavers at the top of the slew in this way whenever you reach the tip of one at the bottom.

As this weave goes alternately in front of one stake and behind the next, an uneven number of stakes is needed to work it continuously, so one was left out in the staking up.

Shape the basket as you work by pulling outwards on the stakes until the required size is achieved. Then keep them straight.

At a height of about 14cm (5½in), finish the slewing and work a set of larch waling, followed by a set of balsam poplar.

4 Here the basketmaker is sitting on the plank to work the border, with the basket on a lapboard *(picture)*. If you have not yet got down on the floor, do try it! It is by far the most comfortable and convenient working position. Sit on a cushion and support your back against a wall. Materials can be laid out on one side, and tools on the other. The basket can be laid on its side and held between the knees for the bottom wale, and then put on a lapboard for the siding and border.

5 The border is a four-rod behind one, worked as on page 19, but bringing each upright down behind one only.

It is finished off by threading the stakes through in correct sequence, and not by cramming off. Each stake to be threaded goes under the elbow of the upright, and out on top of the wale.

It has a follow-on trac to add strength, as the border stakes are a little thin *(picture)*.

Lift up three stakes, and thread the left-hand one to the inside through the gap underneath the right-hand stake.

Move one stake to the right and repeat. The stake goes between the top wale and the border each time.

Continue round the basket, using a bodkin to make spaces for the final three.

6 Handle bows can be shaped in advance, tied with string and allowed to dry, before using them.

Ease a rod gently over your knee and bend it into shape. Leave a long enough length below the curve at the butt end to reach well down the side of the basket.

Mark the places for the handle, to the left of two directly opposite stakes.

Slype both ends of the bow, and insert it as far as you can into the siding, using a greased bodkin to make a space.

Make a slit or hole in the handle bow below the wale on each side, using knife or bodkin *(picture)*.

7 Cut two pieces of willow the size of matchsticks to act as pegs.

Tap a peg into each slit, and trim it off so that it lodges against the wale to hold the bow in place, without protruding too much *(picture)*.

Pick off the whole basket smoothly.

8 The Ash bow handle complements the symmetry of the basket.

# HEDGEROW TRAY

SHEILA WYNTER

A COMBINATION OF several woods gives interest to this basket. There are the soft quiet colours and matt textures of snowberry and wild clematis to contrast with glossy red willow and the purple blue of violet willow. The decorations have been left on the woods, with the willow buds making a fine show.

Scent is as important as appearance, and the violet willows smell pleasantly aromatic.

Getting the sets of prepared material cut, sorted, colour-matched, and counted out is probably the most time-consuming part of hedgerow basketmaking. The actual making of the basket is very much a matter of last minute choices, using the material which is 'kind' at a particular time.

If you do not have a selection of hedgerow woods to use, this tray would make up beautifully with any combination of unstripped, buff, or white cultivated willow.

*Diameter 33cm (13in); Height 12cm (4½in)*

## MATERIALS AND EQUIPMENT

● *8 bottom sticks, 38cm (15in) long and a little thicker than a pencil. Violet (S. daphnoides)* and *yellow willow (S. alba) were used to make a pattern on the slath* ● *1 or 2 pieces of wild clematis* (Clematis vitalba) *to tie the slath, prepared by steaming in a saucepan of hot water, and then peeling (any long fine material would be suitable)* ● *Longish rods of moderate thickness to weave the base, violet and yellow willow* ● *32 stakes of violet willow, carefully chosen, ensuring an even-sized and good-tempered rod to border down* ● *6 walers for upsett, yellow willow* ● *32 matched rods for French rand, snowberry, 30cm (12in) long* ● *6 matched violet willow rods for top wale* ● *Knife* ● *Secateurs* ● *Bodkin* ● *Rapping iron* ● *Hoop* ● *Weight*
. . . . . .

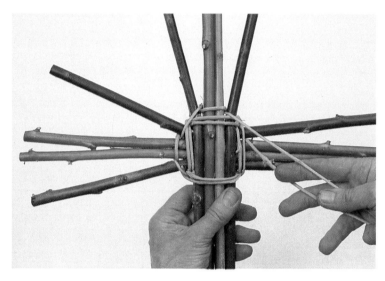

1 Pierce four bottom sticks and thread four through, arranging the sticks to show a colour pattern. Alternate butts and tips.

Loop a strand of wild clematis round the slath, work two rows of pairing round four groups.

Open out the slath, by pairing round the next single bottom stick, and round subsequent sticks in pairs. This produces an octagonal shape. Pair over the last stake with the first of the next round *(picture)*.

2 Work a repeat round of this, and then open out the sticks into singles.

Finish the length of clematis with pairing *(picture)*.

3 Work about six rows of pairing in yellow willow, starting and finishing with tips.

Work one set of waling in violet willow *(picture)*.

4 Work two sets of waling in yellow willow.

Finish with one round of pairing in violet willow.

Crown the base slightly. The tray should be flat when finished, and a slight crown is needed to prevent it from curving the wrong way when staked up.

Pick off the base smoothly, and cut off end sticks (picture).

Stake up on the concave side of the crown.

Slype the 32 violet willow rods on the back, and insert them well in, one on each side of a bottom stick, slype downwards.

Make a space with the bodkin if

necessary. The backs of the rods are towards the inside of the basket, with the slypes showing.

Turn the base over, convex side uppermost, and prick up.

Bend the stakes up and tie them together, or put on a hoop about the size of the base.

5 Work a three-rod wale as a foot track, starting with tips as described in the Egg Basket. Work a second set, finishing with tips. Take off the string or hoop.

The siding is worked in French randing, with one randing rod for every stake. Each row is complete in itself.

The depth of the band of randing depends on the length of the shortest rod, so match them carefully.

Rest the butt of a randing rod inside a stake, and weave it to the right, outside one stake and inside the next, bringing it out in the next space along.

Repeat with a second rod, resting its butt against the stake one place to the left of the first *(picture)*.

6 Work till you reach the last two spaces. Each new butt is put in one place to the left.

Push up the first two randing rods, so that you can see where to put in the last two. *(Picture shows last two held in place.)*

Start each row where you like. It helps to mark the first rod of each round, to remind you to push it and its left-hand neighbour up, so that you can complete the last two strokes of the round more easily. The rows must not cross each other.

Work complete rows until the shortest stake will not go any further.

Finish with a set of waling in violet willow.

7 This is a simple trac border, where each stake in turn is bent down and passes inside one stake, outside two, inside one, outside two again, and finishes inside.

Each stake has to be bent down high enough to allow six other stakes between it and the top wale, so find six pieces similar in size to the border stakes, and use them to help you kink down the first six stakes at the correct height *(picture)*.

Weave the first six stakes into place, keeping a decreasing gap between them and the top wale.

8 From the seventh stake onwards, kink each stake as you go, over the previous ones, keeping them level. There will be no gap between border and wale.

Work until six stakes are still standing up.

Continue to kink and weave away the stakes in the correct sequence. Push them well down onto the top wale as they reach it, to keep a clear space for the next stake.

When you have kinked each stake, lay it along the border and kink it in each of the places where it will have to go in or out. This makes it much easier to thread into position without kinking in the wrong place.

Pick off each border tip on the inside, where it rests against a stake.

Pick off the rest of the basket smoothly.

9 This is a deep tray and makes an attractive and practical container.

# SPIRALLING CANE BOWL

ALEX BURY

THIS BOWL demonstrates some of the possibilities of colour and pattern inherent in the use of dyed cane. Its simple shape provides the setting for the illusion of movement, created by the use of certain dyeing and weaving techniques.

The colours shimmer, and the basket seems to spin like a wheel as you look at it. A wale, worked first in the normal way and then as a reverse wale, gives a lovely zig-zag motion. This movement is heightened by using contrasting colours, and a long stroke – in this case three- and four-rod wale, worked on the inside of the basket. The bowl is a shallow one, and the less interesting back of the weave hardly shows.

The bowl is worked in two colours, plain and dip-dyed. Dip-dyeing one of the colour groups, which causes a variation of colour along its length, adds to the shimmering effect, reminiscent of a traditional Ikat-dyed fabric.

The colours for this piece were inspired by a piece of African textile.

*Base diameter: 15cm (6in); Top edge diameter: 40cm (15½in);*
*Depth 6cm (2½in)*

47

## MATERIALS AND EQUIPMENT

Prepare the materials as on page 9.

Dyed deep red: ● 8 bottom sticks 21cm (8½in) long, No. 11 centre cane ● 32 stakes 52cm (20½in) long, No. 8 centre cane ● 32 by-stakes 20cm (8in) long, No. 8 centre cane ● 225gm (8oz) weavers, No. 5 centre cane

Dip-dyed deep gold: ● 125gm (5oz) weavers, No. 5 centre cane ● 140cm (55in) length border core, No. 16 centre cane

(The border core was dip-dyed so that it would show up clearly against the border stakes. It could be dyed the same colour as the stakes if preferred.)

● Side cutters or shears
● Knife ● Fine bodkin
● Round-nosed pliers

. . . . . .

1 Make up the dye baths as described on page 11, and coil the cane into manageable bundles. Then immerse the material to be dyed red until the required intensity is reached *(picture)*.

For dip-dyeing, dip different sections of the coil into the colour until the required intensity is reached.

Rinse the red cane if you prefer, and drain thoroughly, but do not rinse the dip-dyed cane.

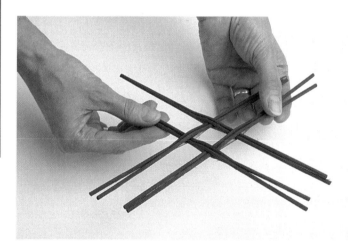

2 The neat, close centre to this bowl is sometimes called a Swedish slath.

Split the centres of the eight stakes with the bodkin, opening up the slits a little.

Lay two sticks out vertically side by side, thread two others through them horizontally as far as the slits.

Thread another pair vertically through the last pair, on the right of the first.

Thread the final pair horizontally over the first vertical pair, and through the second, lying above the first horizontal pair *(picture)*.

Ease all the sticks closely together.

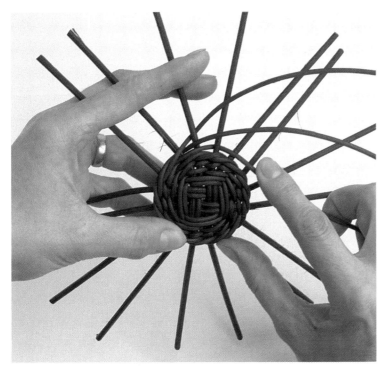

3 Loop a red weaver round an arm of the slath, and tie it in with two rounds of pairing over four sticks.

Open out with one round of pairing over two sticks, followed by one row over single sticks.

Insert a third weaver on the right, and work a row of wale, followed by a row of reverse wale.

Change the stroke as described on page 22 *(picture)*. Work two rows wale, two rows reverse wale, then one row of wale, crowning away from you as you weave.

Keep all white, cut ends on the underneath by starting and finishing weavers behind a stake.

Thread the weavers into the row below, and pick off.

Pick off the bottom sticks close to the weave.

4 Turn the base concave side up. Slype and insert 32 stakes, one on each side of the sticks, slype uppermost. Push well in.

Pinch all stakes with the round-nosed pliers close to the weave, and bend away from you towards the crown, but do not tie them up.

On the concave side, insert four red weavers to the left of four consecutive stakes, and work a foot track of four-rod wale *(picture)*. Fasten off the weavers by threading away in sequence.

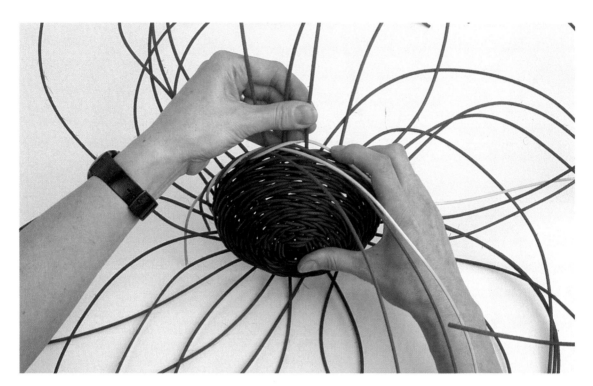

5 Turn the base over. The bowl is worked from the inside, and a wide, shallow flow is created by supporting the stakes at the required angle as you weave.

Insert four weavers into consecutive spaces, alternating red and dip-dyed *(picture)*.

Work three rows of four-rod wale, then change to reverse wale for one row.

Insert by-stakes, one to the right of each stake.

Work two more rows of reverse wale, then four rows of wale.

Change the weaving order to two red, two dip-dyed, and work four rows reverse wale, four rows wale, two rows reverse, and one row wale.

Use the change of stroke, and change the colour order by cutting and replacing canes as unobtrusively as possible.

6 Cut off the by-stakes, and use the pliers to pinch the stakes close to the weaving.

Lay the border core against the edge of the basket with the slyped end projecting a little way to the left. Do not cut it to length yet.

Bring each stake in turn forward over the core, past the next two stakes on the right, and under the core above the weave *(picture)*.

As the border is being worked over it, bring the core ends together, trim and slype the ends to fit. The join is held in place by the wrapping, but it could be glued.

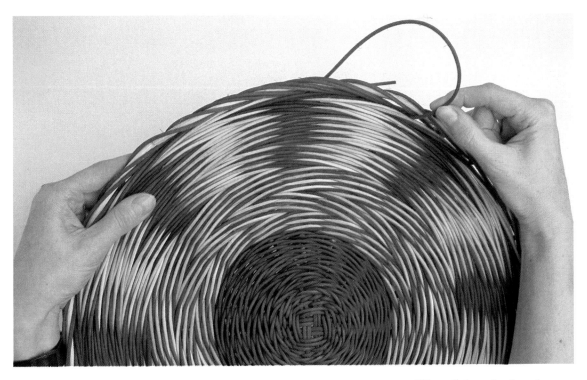

7 When all the stakes have been threaded through, repeat the sequence *(picture)*.

The border cane will not be completely covered.

A third wrap could be worked if the stakes are long enough.

Cane tends to shrink a little as it dries, so wait till the bowl is dry before trimming off all ends where they rest against a stake.

8 Whether hanging on the wall, or used as a container the colour effect is dramatic.

# RUSH BOATER

OLIVIA ELTON BARRATT

THIS HAT combines three of the simplest rushwork techniques: checkweave for the crown, sides, and brim; pairing for the hat band and brim edge; and a two-rod border. It is easy to make, and relies for its effect on the colour and texture of the rush.

Rush hats are worn as sun hats, for gardening, even to weddings, but they are particularly popular with Morris dancers and country dancers, who wear them in many different styles. Bowlers, boaters, toppers, Tyrolean brims, trilbys, and tricornes are all in demand. They can be made to any size or style, with a brim as wide or as narrow as you please.

Many dancers wear them decorated with ribbons or flowers, miniature corn dollies, and badges of all kinds. The self-stick towelling grip designed for squash racket handles makes an excellent interior headband, both for comfort and to hold the hat on.

*To fit average head: Crown depth 9cm (3¹/2in); Brim width: 7.5cm (3in)*

~

## MATERIALS AND EQUIPMENT

● *About 40 large rushes, prepared as on page 10* From these cut about 24 stakes from the butts, saving the ends for weaving.

Stakes should measure:

Twice the allowance for border     25cm (10in)

Twice the width of brim           15cm (6in)

Twice the depth of crown          18cm (7in)

Once across crown approx.         20cm (8in)

Total length      78cm (31in)

● *A hat block, or mould* It is sometimes possible to find wooden millinery blocks in junk shops, but if you are not lucky enough to have one it is easy to make your own out of newspapers. You will need: ● *4 or 5 large newspapers* ● *Masking tape or sellotape* If using a newspaper block, you will need nails about 2.5cm (1in) or longer instead of tacks.

● *Large-headed tacks, about 1.5cm (½in)* ● *Hammer* ● *Rush threader* ● *Scissors with sharp point, for trimming*
. . . . . .

1 Measure your head around the forehead.

Open the newspapers out flat.

Using three sheets at a time, fold them in half lengthwise, three or four times, to make strips about 9cm (3½in) wide.

Crease the folds crisply, and tape them together at each end.

Fold over about 4cm (1½in) at one end, and roll up very tightly to form a rounded oval. Secure with tape.

Secure the next strip to the coil with tape, wrap it tightly round, and secure the other end.

Add strips, pulling very tightly, until you have an oval drum shape 9cm (3½in) deep, and the size of your head measurement. Tape across the block to hold it together. It should feel really solid.

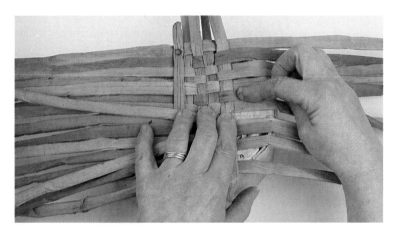

2 You need enough stakes to cover the top of the block.

Lay out enough stakes, butt to tip, to cover length of block, and fasten on across the centre with tacks or nails through a strip of rush.

Weave in stakes across these in checkweave, over one stake and under the next. Alternate butts and tips, and pull and stretch every stake to tighten the weave *(picture)*.

Work from centre to each end.

3 Bring the stakes closer together as you weave, to keep them all within the oval shape.

Where the stakes cross on the corners, pull them firmly into a rounded shape so that they all fit on top of the block. Secure with tacks or nails *(picture)*.

4 Weave in a new rush along the front, with one end forming an extra stake. Knot this end to mark the start of the round *(picture)*.

5 Use this rush to start the siding, weaving round the block over one stake and under the next. Turn the block on its side, crown towards you, and keep pulling the stakes vertically away from you to tighten the weave.

Join in new rushes when necessary, by the tips. Break off the thinnest part and tuck the tip under the old butt for several stakes *(picture)*.

6 When the bottom of the block is reached, add a second weaver. Wrap the tip around a stake so that it goes with the old weaver, with its long end on the right. Weave the tip away with the old weaver *(picture)*.

Work a tight round of pairing for the hat band, using the cut-off ends, and joining where necessary, see page 24.

Thread one of the weavers away into the siding with the lacing tool.

7 Lay the block flat on the table, and spread out all the stakes evenly round it.

Use the remaining weaver to start the checkweave brim *(picture)*.

8 Work six or seven rounds of checkweave, till the brim is just over 7.5cm (3in) wide. Pull the stakes firmly outwards with each stroke to close up the weave.

Overlap joins by several stakes.

Add a weaver and work a row of pairing round the edge, using the cut-off ends *(picture)*.

Thread away both weavers with the tool.

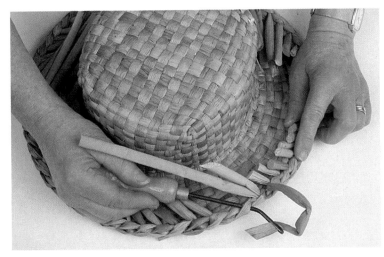

9 Work a two-rod behind one border, bringing down two stakes only to start with, and making up to two pairs.

Finish by threading away the last two stakes in sequence *(picture)*. (Some of the stakes have been cut short for clarity.)

Remove the tacks or nails, and rub your finger-nail over the holes to make them disappear. Allow the hat to dry on the block.

Trim the stakes closely against the border, trim all other ends.

10 A firmly made rush hat is very sturdy and will survive every kind of use for many years.

# RUSH BOX IN
# DIAGONAL WEAVE

OLIVIA ELTON BARRATT

DIAGONAL WEAVE, or plaiting, is a technique used in many different countries in the world to provide strong, light and beautiful structures.

The methods used are similar, whether it is done in cedar or birch bark from Scandinavia, fine strips of split cane from the East, palm leaves from the Carribean, or rushes from Britain. The weave is just right for the suppleness of the rushes, and it shows off their beautiful texture and colours. It can be used to great effect in modern materials too, cardboard strips, leather, webbing, or plastic lending themselves well to the techniques.

The possibilities of diagonal weave for both structure and pattern are excitingly wide. Plain or twill patterns can exploit the use of colour, and it can be worked flat, or three-dimensionally for many different forms.

*Base: 7.5cm (3in) square; Height: 7.5cm (3in)*

~

## MATERIALS AND EQUIPMENT

● *40 medium-sized rushes, 20 for box, 20 for lid, prepared as on page 10* Cut the stakes from the butt ends of these. The length of the stakes should be five times the diagonal of the mould.

● *A wooden mould. A 7.5cm (3in) cube was used here* A really rigid cardboard box would do, stuffed tightly with newspaper, but wood is best.

● *Broad-headed tacks*
● *Hammer* ● *Pair of sharp pointed scissors*

. . . . . .

1 Cover the base with checkweave running diagonally corner to corner, and secure it with tacks.

There must be the same, even number of stakes in both directions – in this case, 10 each way.

There must be a stake on each side of every corner, and it must be the same stake at diagonally opposite corners *(picture)*. Put in tacks to hold the rushes on each side of every corner. These will help you to turn the corners correctly.

2 Start to weave at a corner, by crossing the stakes on each side of it over one another in their correct weaving sequence of over one, under one.

The right-hand corner stake is now pointing diagonally to the left. Weave it up towards the top edge *(picture)*. Pull the stakes to tighten the weave at every stroke.

3 Take the next stake on the right of the corner, and weave it up to the left alongside the first.

Continue to weave the stakes from the right across to the left, until the second corner is reached.

Pull the stakes from both sides in towards the corner, to make them cross each other at right angles.

Turn the second corner like the first, by crossing the two corner stakes over each other in the correct sequence (picture).

4 Continue to weave, pulling it tight as you go, until the weaving has reached the top of the mould.

Stop when there is a stake coming up from the right crossing on top of one coming up from the left (picture).

5 Bring the stake from the left out
from underneath the right-hand
one.

Fold it away from you and down
to the right, to lie on top of the
right-hand stake. It must lie under
at least three of the stakes pointing
to the right for security after
trimming *(picture)*.

Weave the next stake up from the
right, and bring the left-hand one
out from underneath it. Fold the
left-hand one down on top of the
right, as before.

There is a stake sticking up on the
left for every one folded down to
the right.

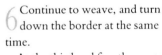

6 Continue to weave, and turn
down the border at the same
time.

At the third and fourth corners,
make sure that you cross the same
pairs of stakes as on their diagonally
opposite corners.

When the border is nearly
complete, you will have to use the
lacing tool to thread the folded-
down stakes through the weave.

If you have turned your corners
correctly, the border will work out
exactly, with one stake turned
down to the right for every one
projecting to the left at the top.

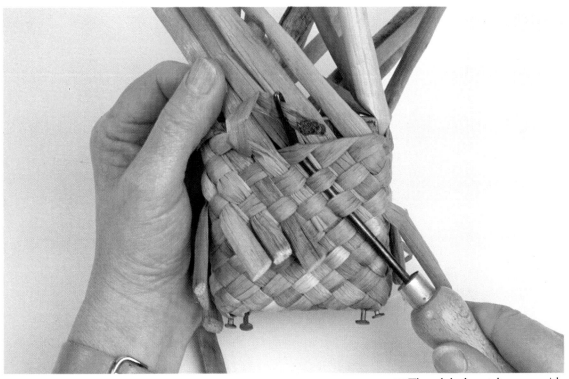

7 Thread the last stake away with the tool *(picture)*.

Pull ends of all projecting stakes to tighten weave, and folded-down ones to tighten top edge.

Take out all the tacks, and rub the holes with your finger-nail to close them.

Dry box on the mould, and cut off all the stakes when dry. Give outside stakes a little pull, trim close to the weave for a neat finish.

Make the lid on top of the box for a good fit. Start the border when the lid is deep enough.

Trim inside stakes at the same angle as the weave after removing box from block.

8 A rush box makes an ideal gift.

# FRAME BASKET

MARY BUTCHER

THIS BASKET is an introduction to frame basket-making, using the simplest possible oval shape. Brown willow is used, which gives the possibility of a wide variety of colours and textures. The willows used here are a variety of *S. alba* to give a coloured stripe, and *S. triandra,* Black Maul.

Frame baskets were usually made for local use, using local materials. Gypsy fruit pickers in many countries used to make frame baskets for their own use and to sell, and in Europe this practice still continues. A local basketmaker might make a very limited range of shapes, and the type of design would depend on the maker and on the locally available material.

Stake and strand basketmakers usually received some training, but frame basketmakers were not part of any formal training structure.

The techniques would have been carried to the New World by the early settlers, and a great variety of frame baskets are found across North America.

*Width: 29cm (11½in); Length: 41cm (16in)*

~

65

## MATERIALS AND EQUIPMENT

Prepare the material as described on page 9.

● *2 thick rods (about thumb thickness) 2.1m (7ft) brown willow for rim and handle hoops (have some spares for emergencies)* ● *8 rods (about little finger thickness) 51cm (20in) long brown willow for ribs or cut from 1.8m (6ft) rods* ● *1kg (2lb) fine weavers in 92–120cm (3–4ft) rods* ● *Some prepared willow skeins, see page 78* or ● *A length of chair cane, fine twine, or fine wire, to bind the hoop* You can use hedgerow materials, but willow is easiest.

● *Shears* ● *Knife* ● *Bodkin*
. . . . . .

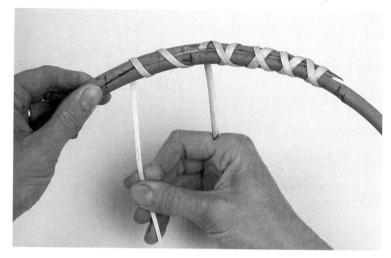

1 The basket's shape depends on the top rim and handle hoops. Make these and leave them to dry, to avoid distortion as you work. Handle is a 29cm (11½in) circle, rim a 41cm (16in) oval.

Slype the butt of a rod on the belly, for about 12cm (5in).

Rest the middle of the rod against your stomach or over your knee, and curve it into a circle. Work it carefully to shape and size.

Overlap the ends, and mark them at the beginning, middle and end of the slype.

To bind the hoop, put the tail of the binder through the centre of the overlap. Bind to the end of the slype in one direction, and back to the centre, spacing out the wraps *(picture)*.

Bind to the other end of the slype and back to the centre.

Pull the binder through the slit beside the tail.

2 Mark positions for the handle at halfway points on the rim.

Starting with the tip of a weaver on the inside of the handle pointing downwards to the right, wrap the weaver on the outside diagonally downwards across the join to the right, securing its own tip.

Bring it behind the lower handle hoop, up to the right across the join, then back down under the rim and over the lower handle hoop *(picture)*.

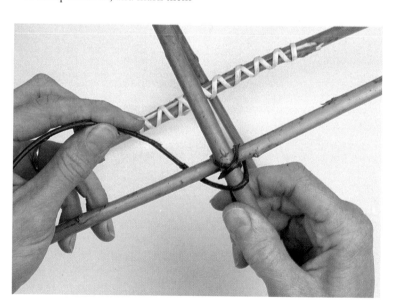

3 Weave in and out over the rim and the lower half of the handle, working from side to side.

Join in a new rod by laying the butt against the lower handle hoop *(picture)*. Work out to the tip.

Repeat on the other side.

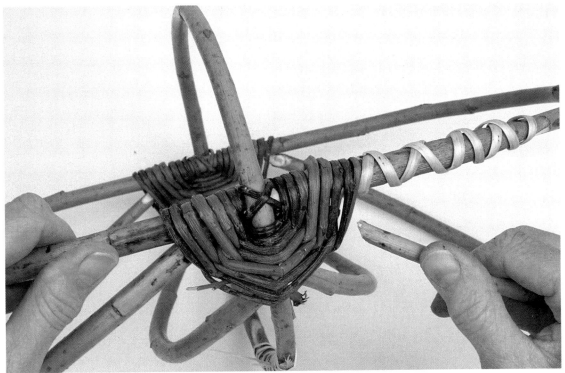

4 Cut two ribs for each side, matching the lengths. Slype the ends on the belly and push them well into the weave on either side of the handle join *(picture)*.

The ribs determine the silhouette of the basket. Long ribs towards the rim give it length, shorter ones near the handle hoop keep it flat. The long ribs here were 50cm (19½in) and the shorter ones 33cm (13cm).

Weave in four more rods on each side, making a full turn round the rim each time you go round it from now on.

Keep the joins on the centre ribs.

If you have them, put in two weavers of a different colour on each side, starting and finishing with tips.

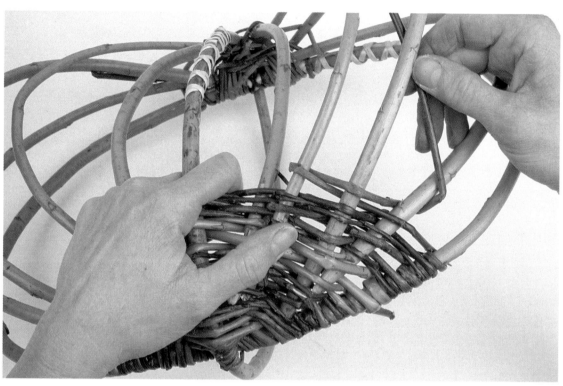

5 Put in the two remaining ribs on each side. One goes between the hoop and the first rib, another between the first and second ribs.

Check on the shape and adjust the rib length if necessary.

Weave for six more rods each side, spacing the ribs very carefully.

The weaving must be 'packed', to level the gap in the centre. When you reach the third rib after going over the rim, turn back and weave to the rib nearest the rim. Turn back again, weave to other side *(picture)*.

Do this every time you go over the rim until the gap is level.

6 Weave on each side in turn until the middle gap is filled.

Thread the last few weavers in carefully to fill the gap, ending sequence. Pick off all ends inside where they rest against a stake.

7 An alternative method of tying the hoops together is to use the God's Eye, a decorative cross used in many countries.

Lay the tip of a weaver, skein, or piece of chair cane on the outside of the handle join, pointing diagonally down to the left.

Bring the weaver behind the upper part of the handle from the right, over it and diagonally down to the right, securing its tip, under the rim, then up behind it.

Bring the weaver diagonally down to the left, across and then behind the lower handle hoop.

Continue this move around the tie until there is a substantial cross over handle and rim.

Tuck the end of the weaver into the wraps on the handle bow.

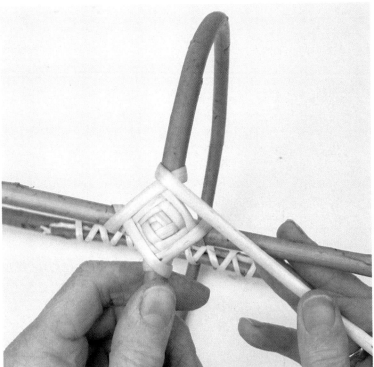

8 The natural shape of the frame basket is one of its great charms.

# BROWN AND WHITE WILLOW DOG BASKET

### JONATHAN GORDON

THIS OVAL dog basket is the smallest of a set of five, designed to stack one inside the other. Piles of these baskets nesting inside each other make a delightful sight at country fairs and craft markets. This is a very traditional design in brown and white willow, with a notch in the front for the dog to step in.

The basket has the traditional English oval slath, made under the feet instead of piercing the bottom sticks. The border is a four-rod behind two.

Slewing is used for the base and siding. This is a weave much used by commercial basketmakers, because it can be worked with tops and leftovers from other baskets, making it very economical.

The combination of brown and white willow is a favourite with basketmaker and customer alike, and the use of white for the top half gives this basket balance and visual appeal.

*Base: 33×48cm (13×19in); Top: 41×56cm (16×22in);*
*Height at back: 23cm (9in); Height at front: 20cm (8in)*

## MATERIALS AND EQUIPMENT

Prepare the materials as described on page 9.

Approx. quantities: ● *60 rods 1.8–2.1m (6–7ft) brown willow for bottom sticks, slath rods, stakes and walers* ● *50 rods 92–120cm (3–4ft) brown willow* ● *12 rods 92–120cm (3–4ft) white willow* ● *2 25cm (10in) thick sticks for notch posts (Pieces of thick straight ash or hazel from the hedge would do)* ● *Knife* ● *Secateurs* ● *Bodkin* ● *Rapping iron* ● *Weight*
. . . . . .

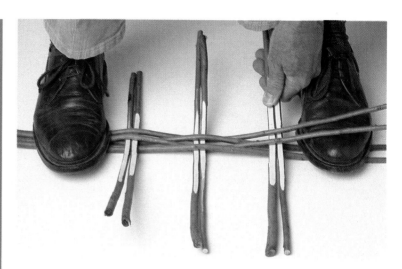

1 Slype six 38cm (15in) bottom sticks across the centre on the bellies.

Hold the butts of four slath rods under your right foot, tips on left.

Lift up the front and third from front rods.

Lay two bottom sticks, slype upwards, in the gap, about half their own length from the rod butts.

Let down the first two rods, and pick up the other two.

Put in two more bottom sticks about 10cm (4in) from the first.

Repeat to put in the last two sticks *(picture)*.

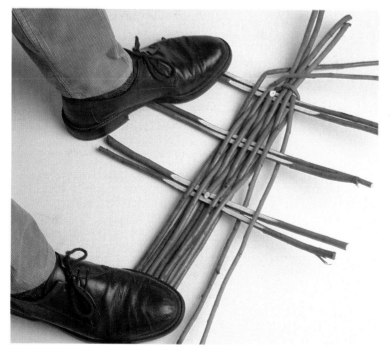

2 Lay in a short extra stick under the central pair, resting on the outside pairs.

Hold the other end of the slath down with the left foot, and lay in four more slath rods in sequence, butts to the left, projecting as far as the first ones. Press closely together.

On the left, lift the slath rod nearest the short stick. Bend its left-hand neighbour under the four butts and out to the front.

Pair round the next two shoulder sticks, rand over the middle two, and bring the lower rod up behind the next two.

Repeat with the second pair of slath rods *(picture)*.

3 Turn base, repeat at other end. Pair round each end in turn, dividing the bottom sticks into singles, except for a pair at one end only, to leave an uneven number.

Rand over central ones together.

Work out to tips of slath rods.

Work a four-rod slew with small brown willow, pulling up each shoulder to give a crown.

Start with one rod at the left shoulder, and build up to four.

When adding a new butt, trap it on top of a stake with the slewing rods, before bringing it to the outside of the group *(picture)*.

Make base to the required size.

Finish with a round of pairing in large brown willow, started by slyping the butts and pricking them down into the weave. At the end of the round, thread the weavers away and pick off.

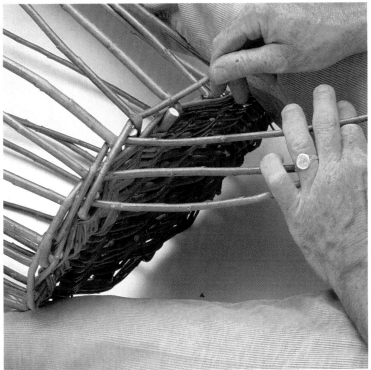

4 Slype 29 rods on the back. The back of the rods will be inwards, and the slypes will show.

With the concave side of the base uppermost, drive the stakes in slype downwards, using single stakes for the two front straight shoulder sticks, and for three of the sticks at one end. (Avoid the end with the undivided pair.)

Start a four-rod wale at each end, slyping the butts and pricking them down into the weave *(picture)*.

When each wale reaches the start of the other one, drop one rod and continue with three. Keep the two wales separate. They follow one another round.

Work one more complete set of three-rod wale.

5 Using small brown willow, work 7.5cm (3in) of four-rod slew, allowing the basket to flow out a little, particularly at the ends.

Slype and insert the notch posts about 18cm (7in) apart, on the left of the stakes on the two front straight shoulder sticks.

Start a three-rod wale at the back with the tips of large brown willow, work round to the notch, and bring down the stakes between the posts in a three-rod behind one border *(picture)*.

Finish the wale at the back.

6 Using the white willow, work a three-rod slew to 20cm (8in) at the back. Rap down in front to 18cm (7in). There is no top wale.

Lay two large rods in first two spaces to right of post, with about 25cm (10in) of butts to the inside.

Bring the right-hand butt round in front of the post and first upright stake, behind the next two stakes, and out to the front. Bring the first upright down behind the next two to make a pair *(picture)*.

Bring the left-hand butt round the post, in front of three uprights,

behind one and out. Bring the second upright down with it to make a pair.

Continue in a four-rod behind two border until three stakes are left upright.

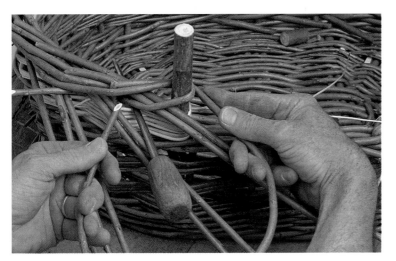

7 Bring the next pair down in
front of post. The next upright
comes down in the same place.

The left-hand horizontal goes in
front of the final upright, behind
and round the post, back to the
inside over the final pair, then out
again in the next space along.

The final upright goes round the
post below the previous one,
through to the inside, and back to
the outside in next space *(picture)*.

Pick off the whole basket. Cut
off posts level with the border.

8 Slype a large rod and insert it
next to the post.

Starting at the tip, twist and roll
it with both hands to break up the
fibres, and then twist and wind
down the length of the rod. This
makes it possible to treat it a bit like
string. It takes practice, and you
may have to replace the rod and try
again!

Wind the rod up into a firm rope
and thread it over the white willow
slew and below the wale to the
inside.

Bring it twice over the border
and through the wale in the same
place *(picture)*.

Bring it over the border and
under its own wraps on the outside,
around the post, and thread it away
into the weave.

Repeat on other side.

9 The size of the basket can be
varied to suit the dog or cat.
This basket has one fewer stakes
between the notch posts.

# FRUIT BASKET IN
# UNSTRIPPED WILLOW

JENNY CRISP

JENNY'S DESIGNS evolve through an understanding of traditional basketmaking techniques, and a response to the qualities of the material. All her baskets are made of English willow from her own willow bed or from the Somerset levels, and growing the willows gives her a deeper insight and greater sympathy with the material and the baskets she makes.

Fitching and scalloming are two traditional French techniques which she learnt early on in her apprenticeship, and this basket evolves from her response to these techniques, and from the need to develop her own designs. Her aim is to bring together the intrinsic qualities of willow to create an object whose beauty is the natural consequence of its composition and function.

Her chosen design is an openwork fruit basket, a form of frame basket, with an open fitched base and sides, and a wide border. It is made entirely of unstripped willow.

*Diameter: 28cm (11in); Depth: 11cm (4½in)*

~

## MATERIALS AND EQUIPMENT

Prepare the materials as described on page 9.

● *1 willow rod 2.4–2.7m (8–9ft) for hoop, straight and no blemishes* ● *From a bolt of 1.2m (4ft) brown willow: approx. 30 thick rods cut to 33cm (13in) for bottom sticks; approx. 10 finest rods for fitching and waling; approx. 50 medium rods for stakes, with scallomed butts; a few fine rods to make willow skeins* ● *Knife* ● *Secateurs* ● *Rapping iron* ● *Weight* ● *Bodkin* ● *Second bodkin to pin work to lapboard*

. . . . . .

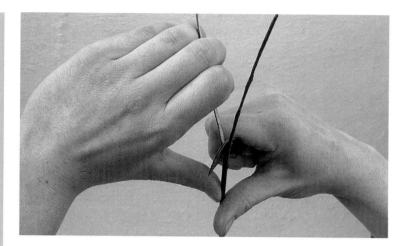

1 Skeins are thin ribbons of willow made by splitting a rod, here used to tie the hoop, and to tie the ends of the bottom sticks on to it.

Use your knife to split the tip of a fine rod for about 2.5cm (1in). Then use both knife and hands to split the rod along its length, using pressure to one side or the other to keep the split running evenly. (Some people find it easier to split the rod from the butt.)

Scrape carefully with your knife to remove the pith and produce a thin, flat skein.

Re-dip in water before use.

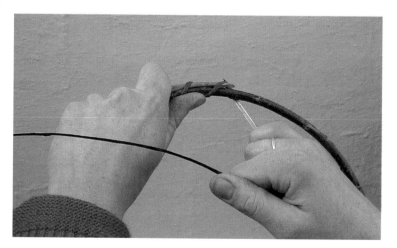

2 Starting with the butt, shape the thick rod against the natural curve, bending it around your knee, and easing it into a circle of the required size.

Overlap it by about 15cm (6in).

Slype the outside of the tip and the inside of the butt to fit together, with the butt (the stronger) on the outside.

Trap the end of the skein between butt and tip, and use it to bind the hoop, pulling the butt end in firmly *(picture)*.

Tuck the end of the skein away.

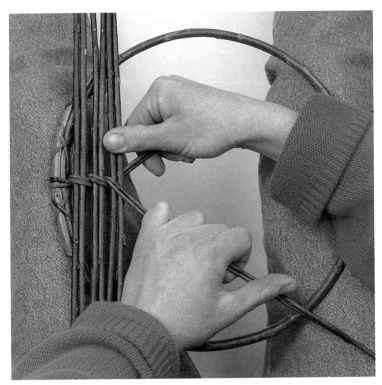

3 Attach the sticks to the hoop with fitching – similar to a row of reverse pairing – using two fine rods butt to tip, to give one weaver of even thickness.

Wrap the halved rods at their centre around the hoop, to give two weavers.

Holding the left weaver in the left hand, push it under, and pull the right one over with the right hand. Cross them tightly. Change hands.

Lay a pair of sticks, butt to tip, between the weavers and push them up tight to the twist.

Repeat the fitching stroke, and lay in two more sticks close to the twist *(picture)*.

Continue till the hoop is filled, finishing by turning the fitch rods round the hoop and weaving back for two or three strokes.

4 Tie the ends of the bottom sticks to the hoop with skeins, or whole fine rods.

Trap the tip of a skein between hoop and sticks, and then wrap it both over itself and over the pair of sticks, to tie them to the hoop *(picture)*.

Continue this technique until all the pairs are tied to the hoop, and secure the skein.

Repeat at the other end.

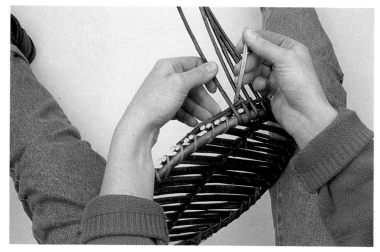

5 All 50 stakes must be scallomed, to secure them to the hoop.
A scallom is a long flexible tongue cut at the butt of a rod, and used as a tie.

Rest the butt end on your chest, with the back upwards and to the right. With the knife, cut down and towards you into the back of the rod, with a rounded movement, about 13cm (5in) from the butt.

Split, rather than cut, towards the butt, using pressure with the thumbs *(picture)*. Finish with a thin tail.

6 Tie on the scallomed rods. Slip the first scallom under the hoop, bring it up just to right of fitch.

Bend rod up against hoop on out-side, and the scallom on the inside.

Bring the scallom out to the right of the stake and wrap it tightly across outside it, and to the left.

Hold it down against the sticks with the left hand.

Set the next stake about two stakes width to the left, and tie it on in the same way, enclosing the scallom from the first stake *(picture)*.

Repeat with subsequent stakes around the frame, enclosing all the scalloms. The final few scalloms are threaded away through the first ones.

7 Mark the stakes at 7.5cm (3in) all round.

Begin the top fitch at this point with two long rods, butt to tip.

About halfway round, replace the butts with new butts, staggering the joins *(picture)*.

Put the new butt down through the last stroke as you make it. Then bring the new rod behind the stake and over to the right of the butt it is to replace.

Make the next stroke with the new rod, leaving the old butt protruding.

8 Complete the round of fitching with the new rods, adding two tips to achieve an even thickness.

At the end of the fitched round, drop the butts, and with the tips make one fitching stroke and one ordinary pairing stroke.

Lay in two butts in the next two spaces *(picture)*.

Work one round of four-rod wale with two tips and two butts, joining where necessary to maintain the thickness.

9 The wide border is a six-rod behind three, threaded away and not crammed.

Kink nine rods at the width of your thumb above the wale, starting on the opposite side to the join in the fitch.

Bring down the first six rods in succession, each one behind three.

Lay the first of these in front of three uprights and behind the next, allowing it to curve out from the wale. Use your thumb to hold this curve in place. The first upright comes down behind the same stake to make a pair, and slips underneath the horizontal one *(picture)*.

Lay the next horizontal in place keeping the same amount of curve *(picture)*. This is to allow room for the final stakes to be threaded away. The left hand holds the uprights back and to the left, to keep the work in position.

10 Continue the border, kinking each stake down level with the others before laying it in place.

At the end of the round, keep working in sequence, threading away the stakes, until all the uprights are down *(picture)*.

The horizontals are all threaded

from inside to outside in sequence, each one going under the elbow of one upright, and under the border stakes already in position.

Each successive upright goes under one more border stake *(picture)*. Pick off all ends.

# OVAL FLOWER AND VEGETABLE BASKET

JOHN GALLOWAY

THIS BASKET IS MADE in buff and white willow dyed with coal-tar indigo, and fibre reactive dyes (though commercial dyes can be used). It has the English traditional underfoot slath, with four pairs of bottom sticks to give it length. The sides are packed with slewing to give an elegant downward sweep to the ends. An interesting feature is the sisal rope worked in under the top wale, and used to cover and tie in the handle, giving strength as well as decoration. The completed basket is scrubbed with water, thoroughly dried, and brushed with linseed oil to give lustre to the willow.

The dye ingredients are dissolved together in hot water, poured into a drain pipe blocked at one end, and topped up with hot water to just over the half way mark for economy and stronger colour. The rods are put in the drain pipe until the desired colour is reached, then removed and inverted to dye the tips. Four colours are used for the sisal rope.

*Base: 25 × 43cm (10 × 17in); Height of handle: 28cm (11in)*
*Height of sides: 15cm (6in)*

~

## MATERIALS AND EQUIPMENT

● *8 bottom sticks, 2.1m (7ft)* ● *9 layers (full length rods) – also called slath rods 1.8m (6ft)* ● *4 for base slewing 1.8m (6ft)* ● *4 for pairing the base 2.1m (7ft)* ● *18 for side stakes 1.8m (6ft)* ● *22 for end stakes 1.5m (5ft)* (the ends are lower than the sides). ● *16 for upsett 1.5m (5ft)* ● *16 for slewed packing 0.9 or 1.2m (3 or 4ft)* ● *6 for top wale 1.8m (6ft)* ● *1 2.75m (9ft) for handle bow (or as thick as possible)* ● *4 lengths of 3-ply sisal rope each approx 1.8m (6ft)* ● *Dyes in four colours* (You could economize with 2 colours and 2 lengths.) ● Knife ● Shears ● Bodkin ● Rapping iron ● Weights ● Raw linseed oil and a soft brush

· · · · · ·

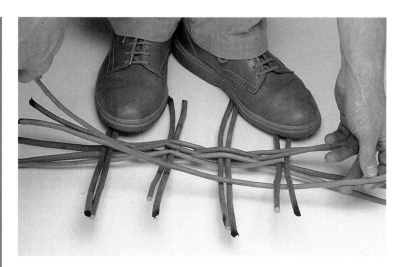

1 Cut four pairs of 30cm (12in) bottom sticks, and lay them out with 25cm (10in) between the end pairs. Standing on the sticks, as shown *(picture)*, weave in four layers with the butts protruding to your right 13cm (5in) from the end pairs. The first layer goes under the right hand pair.

Put a short layer in the centre, with the butt protruding 13cm (5in) from under the right hand sticks, and the tip cut off to rest on the other pair.

Use the layers at each end to tie in the slath and rand down the sides, taking them over or under the butt ends in correct randing sequence.

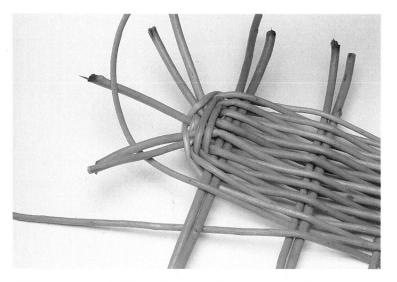

2 Open out the end sticks in three groups, one, two, and one at the end with four butts, two, one, and two at the end with five *(picture)*.

Rand the rods to the opposite ends again, keeping the central sticks as pairs.

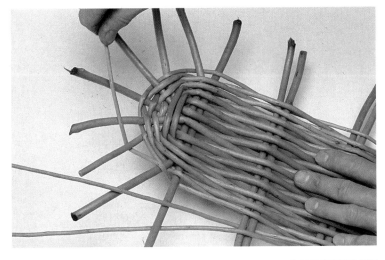

3 Open out the end bottom sticks and the butt ends as singles with randing *(picture)*. Work the layers out to the tips. Keep the inside end sticks straight.

Slew up the base with 1.8m (6ft) rods, introducing a new rod to the slew on each left hand shoulder every time. Work out to 23 × 40cm (9 × 16in), crowning the base slightly.

4 On each side, slype and insert two 2.1m (7ft) rods to the right of the two left hand sticks. Kink them to leave a 2cm (¾in) gap, and pair round, taking each one behind a pair of sticks for the first stroke *(picture)*.

Thread the tips through the gaps on the opposite side, then repeat with the first tips. Cut them off, and pick off the base. Cut off the bottom sticks close to the weave.

Slype the stakes on the belly and insert them with the slype uppermost.

5 Insert eleven 1.5m (5ft) stakes at each end, one on each side of every bottom stick, but missing out one stake at the end with four butts, and three at the end with five.

Insert eight 1.8m (6ft) stakes along each side, treating the central pairs as single sticks.

Add an extra stake in centre on each side *(picture)*. Prick up stakes.

Upsett with a set of four-rod wale, starting with the tips and joining the butts on the shoulder. Work a second set joining the butts on the opposite shoulder.

6 Pack each side separately with slewing using smallest rods.

Starting at the fifth stake to the left of the central one, lay in a butt and rand to the corresponding stake at the other end, adding two more rods. Turn and work back to the left, adding a fourth rod.

Turn again on the first stake, and continue a four-rod slew to and fro on a decreasing number of stakes.

When you are working on seven stakes, tail off the slew. It should be about 12cm (5in) high. Finish over five stakes *(picture)*.

7 Slype and insert handle bow, 28cm (11in) tall to left of central stake on each side.

Separate the rope into strands and use one strand of each colour.

Leaving enough 'tail' to reach from the end of the basket to the handle, plus about 15cm (6in), wrap one strand right across the bow, leaving 2.5cm (1in) gaps between wraps *(picture)*.

Wrap the other strands around the bow in the gaps, keeping them in their correct order and leaving the 'tails' hanging on each side.

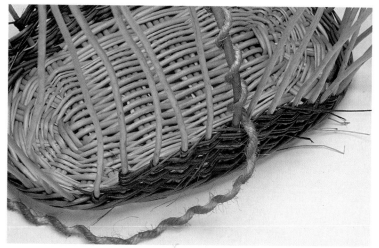

8 The fourth strand should just fill the last gap. Grip the handle and roll the rope round the bow to tighten it.

Using the same pairs of colours on each side of the bow, reverse pair them to each end, with two twists between each stake where there is room. (The twists must slope from top left to bottom right) *(picture)*.

9 Work till the two sets of strands meet at the end of the basket, with one strand from each direction on the outside and one on the inside, and one stake between them.

Bring the inside strand from the right behind this stake and to the outside *(picture)*.

Then replace the other right hand outside strand with the left hand one for three twists. Finish with the left hand strand on the inside and the right one on the outside.

There should be two stakes between the pairs of rope ends.

10 Add one set of three-rod wale with 1.8m (6ft) rods, working round handle bow and stake together. Join the butts at one end.

Rap down the wale firmly.

Starting three stakes to the right of the bow, prick down six stakes 2cm (¾in) above the wale, and work a six-rod behind two border. Curve it away from the basket and downward to allow for threading through.

Work the border around the handle bow *(picture)*.

Thread away the ends as on page 81. Tighten up the first stakes to make the border even.

Pick off the basket and cut the ends of rope short inside and out.

Using the soft brush, scrub the basket with water, dry thoroughly, and brush lightly with raw linseed oil to bring out the colour.

# WILLOW LETTER TRAY

### SALLY GOYMER

THE DESIGN for this letter tray is entirely functional, and while its equivalent in plastic or metal can be found in any office today, it was originally made in willow. It can be modified to include other materials, colour, and weaves, but the simplicity of design and material is enough on its own to produce a work of beauty.

The basket is in square work, and the base is made in the French manner, without a screw block, one of the many techniques which Sally learned at the French National School of Basketry. The time she spent there helped to give her work the precision and polish which characterizes it, and she has her own approach to the classic French designs.

The notch on this letter tray is similar to that on the dog basket, but the border requires some special techniques to produce the square corners.

*Length: 38cm (15in); Width: 25cm (10in); Depth 11cm (4½in)*

## MATERIALS AND EQUIPMENT

Prepare the materials as described on page 9.

● *From a bolt of 1.2m (4ft) willow: approx. 50 fine base weavers, 44 thick side stakes, 41 medium walers, approx. 30 fine side weavers, 5 extra medium rods, for corners and ties* ● *9 base sticks 43cm (17in) long, from 1.8m (6ft) rods* ● *4 corner sticks 11.5cm (4½in) long* ● *2 notch sticks*

The corner and notch sticks can be cut from 1.3cm (½in) dowelling.

● Knife ● Secateurs
● Bodkin ● Rapping iron
● Weight

. . . . . .

1 Tie two pairs of bottom sticks together, butt to tip.

Lay the pairs on a low bench, 25cm (10in) apart, with five sticks between them, butt to tip, half their length protruding over the edge.

Lay a bunch of willows across them to hold them down, and sit astride them to weave.

Rand from the centre with a tip, weaving first under, then over, the right-hand pair. This makes it easier to keep the sticks straight.

Rand to and fro, joining in butts from now on, joins underneath, and turning right round the end sticks to start with for stability *(picture)*. Keep the end sticks parallel.

Work half the base, and thread away the last weaver. Pick off the ends close to the sticks.

Sit on the finished half of the base, and work the second half from the centre in the same way.

Pick off ends. (The smooth side will be inside the basket.)

2 Slype 18 stakes on the belly, and insert them slype downwards in the short ends, nine rods each. (Two stakes for each of the sticks on either side of the centre.)

Prick up stakes, tie together.

Trim four walers to 36cm (14in) and slype two tips and two butts.

On the left, insert two tips right into the outside sticks, and two butts above and below where the sticks touch. Use a greased bodkin to make the spaces.

Start a four-rod wale with a 'pull-down', as shown *(picture)*.

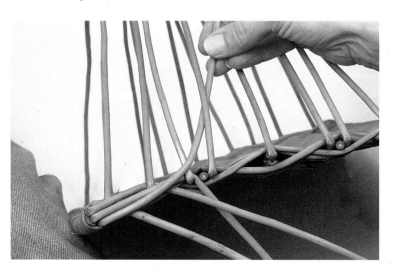

3 When the right-hand waler reaches the end sticks, drop this rod, and cram off the other three to match the left side, using the bodkin to make spaces *(picture)*.

Repeat at the other end.

4 Slype the remaining stakes with a flat cut on the back.

Mark the places for them on the long sides, 13 to each side. Position the outside ones close to the corner.

Starting on the right of each long side, insert a stake slype upwards into the channel between the two outside bottom sticks, using the greased bodkin. Push it in to the end of the slype. Kink it upwards a little distance away, and tap it home with the rapping iron *(picture)*.

Repeat with all the stakes except the last on each side.

Sharpen the last stake on each side, drive it straight down between the bottom sticks, and cut off the point.

Insert four corner sticks in the same way, as much on the corner as possible.

Work four sets of three-rod wale, starting, joining in new butts, and finishing on the short ends.

5 Slype and insert notch posts on a short end, on the left of the third stake in on each side.

Start another wale the other end, and use it to turn down the notch as for the Dog Basket, see page 74. Complete the wale.

Rand backwards and forwards, joining weavers by the butts on the inside, for 10cm (4in). Keep corner stakes close to corner posts.

Start the top wale by looping a butt round the right notch post, and laying in another in the second space along.

Finish by looping the left-hand waler round at the corner post, and threading away beyond the left-hand stake *(picture)*.

6 Trim corner posts level with the wale, and make a hole in each with the bodkin. Slype and insert stakes in the holes. (Alternatively the stakes can be inserted between the weave and the corner post.)

Start a four-rod behind two border exactly as shown for the Dog Basket, see page 74 *(picture)*.

A square corner is worked quite differently for the next few strokes using a 'last in first out' method.

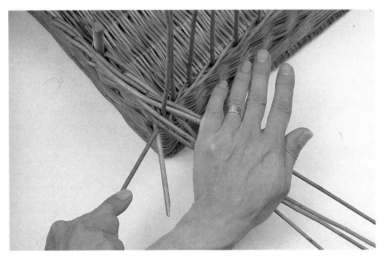

7 With a pair of rods behind the corner stake, bring the last upright before it down into this space as well. The last upright but one lies underneath the other two rods, at a different angle *(picture)*.

Bring the right-hand stake of each of the next three pairs together horizontally, outside the corner, with the right-hand one on the outside – last in.

Kink this one up and over the others, in line with the edge of the basket – first out *(picture)*.

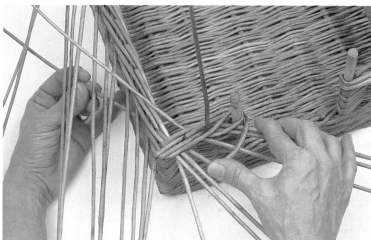

8 This stake goes in front of the corner stake and behind the next one. It does not have a pair.

Bring the next horizontal – second out – stake up and over, along the edge of the basket, and behind the second upright. Bring corner stake down to make a pair.

Bring the last horizontal – last out – stake up and over, behind the third stake, and out. Bring the next upright down to make a pair.

Use right-hand stake of the three in corner for the next stroke, with the next upright *(picture)*.

Use the single horizontal stake for the next stroke, and continue border as normal to next corner.

9 Work to the final corner. 'First out', 'second out', and corner stakes are worked as normal.

'Last out' goes in front of the last upright, then behind the notch post, around to the front, and back to the inside beyond the last upright.

The second from last upright goes behind the notch post below the other rod, round to the front, and back to the inside beyond two stakes. It is threaded right across the corner to make it easier to pull tight *(picture)*.

10 Twist the last upright into a rope and use it to tie the border down, threading it out under the wale from the inside, and then over the border twice, before threading it away into the weave *(picture)*.

Slype a rod and insert it to the left of the stake next to the right-hand notch post, and make the tie.

Trim off the notch posts level with the border.

# USEFUL INFORMATION

THE BASKETMAKERS' ASSOCIATION *Millfield Cottage, Little Hadham, Ware, Hertfordshire. SG11 2ED England.*

THE BASKETMAKER, *M.K.S. Publications Inc. PO Box 340 Westland, Michigan 48185. U.S.A.*

## SUPPLIERS

P.H. COATE AND SON *(Willows), Meare Green Court, Stoke St. Gregory, Near Taunton, Somerset, England.*

R. HECTOR *(Willows), 18 Windmill Hill, North Curry, Nr. Taunton, Somerset, England.*

C. MOLLART *(Willows), Broadwater Farm, Ossington, Newark, Nottinghamshire, NG23 6LN England.*

TOM ARNOLD *(Rushes), Wildcroft, Holywell, St Ives, Huntingdon, Cambridgeshire, PE17 3TG England*

COUNTRY CHAIRMEN *(Rushes), Home Farm, School Road, Ardington, Nr. Wantage, Oxfordshire. England.*

JACOBS YOUNG AND WESTBURY LTD. *(Willow, Rush and Cane), Bridge Road, Haywards Heath, West Sussex, HR16 1TZ England.*

THE CANE STORE *(Willow, Rush, Cane, Tools, Books), 207 Blackstock Road, Highbury Vale, London, N5 2LL England.*

JOHN EXCELL *(Willow Tools, Rush), The Cane Workshop, The Gospel Hall, Westport, Langport, Nr. Ilminster, Somerset, England.*

HAYS CHEMICALS LTD. *(Dyes), 55/57 Glenfall Road, London, SE15 England.*

BRIDON FIBRES *(Sisal Rope), British Ropes Ltd., Anchor and Hope Lane, London, SE7, England.*

ENGLISH BASKETRY WILLOWS *(Willows), RFD1, Box 124a, Dept. A., South New Berlin, New York 13843, U.S.A.*

WALTERS LTD. *(Willows), Mountain Road, Washington Island, 54246, U.S.A.*

THE H.H. PERKINS CO. *(Basketry Supplies, Dyes), 10 South Bradley Road, Woodbridge, Connecticut 06525, U.S.A.*

THE CANING SHOP *(Basketry Supplies, Books), 926 Gilman Street, Berkeley, CA 94710, U.S.A.*

ROYALWOOD LTD *(Basketry Supplies, Willows), 517 Woodville Road, Mansfield, Ohio 44907, U.S.A.*

| CANE SIZES | | |
|---|---|---|
| Thickness in mm | English No. | American No. |
| VERY FINE | | |
| 1.375 | 000 | |
| 1.5 | 00 | 1 |
| 1.625 | 0 | |
| FINE | | |
| 1.75 | 1 | 2 |
| 1.85 | 2 | |
| 2 | 3 | 2½ |
| MEDIUM | | |
| 2.25 | 4 | 3 |
| 2.5 | 5 | 3½ |
| 2.625 | 6 | |
| 2.75 | 7 | 4 |
| 3 | 8 | 4½ |
| THICK | | |
| 3.25 | 9 | 5 |
| 3.33 | 10 | |
| 3.5 | 11 | 5½ |
| 3.75 | 12 | |
| 4 | 13 | 6 |
| 4.35 | 14 | |
| 5 | 15 | 6½ |
| 5.5 | 16 | 7 |
| HANDLE CANE | | |
| 8 | 20 | 10 |
| 9 | 9mm | |
| 10 | 10mm | 12 |
| 12 | 12mm | |

# INDEX

**A**

Africa, 6
American Indians, 6
Argentine, 8

**B**

back, 14
Bamford, Joni, 27
bases, 14, 15
    hedgerow materials, 36
    rushwork, 24
Behennah, Dail, 30
belly 14
block waling, 22–3
blocks, hat, 54
boaters, rush, 52–7
bodkins, 12
bolts, willow, 8–9
borders, 15
    fruit basket, 81
    hedgerow materials, 38
    oval platter, 23–4
    rod borders, 14, 25
    rushwork, 25, 62–3
    shopping basket, 19–20
    trac, 15, 25, 45
bowls, spiralling cane, 46–51
boxes, rush box in diagonal
    weave, 58–63
Bury, Alex, 29, 46–51
Butcher, Mary, 28, 64–9
butt, 14
bye-stakes, 14, 21

**C**

cane, 9
    dyeing, 11
    handling, 15
    oval platter, 21–4
    preparation, 9
    shopping basket, 21
    sizes, 9, 94
    spiralling bowl, 46–51
    Swedish lath, 48
cardboard, 11
centre cane see cane
chain pairing, 22
chain waling, 23
changing the stroke, 14
checkweave, 14, 56–7, 60

Chile, 8
China, 7
cleaves, 12
coiled baskets, 6, 14, 25
colour: dyeing, 11
    hedgerow materials, 47
    spiralling cane bowl, 47–8
cores, coiled baskets, 25
cram, 14, 20
Crisp, Jenny, 31, 76–81
crowns, 14, 15, 17, 43
cutting out, 14

**D**

Dalby, Lee, 32
Dead Sea Scrolls, 6
diagonal weave, 14
    rush box, 58–63
dip-dyeing, 47, 48
dog basket, brown and white
    willow, 70–5
dyeing, 11
    dip-dyeing, 47, 48
    willow, 83

**E**

egg basket in hedgerow
    materials, 34–9
elbow, 14
Elton Barratt, Olivia, 29, 52–63
English rand, 14, 19

**F**

fitching, 14, 77, 79–81
flow, 14
flower basket, 82–7
follow-on trac, 23–4
foot track, 14
football lacers, 12
frame baskets, 14, 25, 64–9,
    76–81
Freitas, John, 31
French National School of
    Basketry, 89
French rand, 14, 89–93
fruit basket in unstripped
    willow, 76–81

**G**

Galloway, John, 28, 82–7
God's Eye, 69
Gordon, Jonathan, 70–5
Goymer, Sally, 32, 88–93
grease horn, 12

**H**

handles: frame baskets, 66
    handle bows, 14, 39
    handle liners, 14, 18
    pegging, 14, 39
    roped, 14, 25, 35
    rushwork, 25
    shopping baskets, 20–1
    sisal rope, 83, 86–7
hats: hat blocks, 54
    rush boater, 52–7
hedgerow materials, 10–11
    egg basket, 34–9
    handling, 15
    preparation, 11
    trays, 40–5
history, 6–7
hoops, 12, 14

**J**

Johnson, Kay, 21–4

**K**

knives, 12

**L**

lapboards, 12, 37
letter tray, willow, 88–93
linseed oil, 83, 87
lipwork, 25

**M**

Manthorpe, Colin, 28
materials, 8–11
measures, 12
mellowing: rushes, 10
    willow, 9
Middle East, 6
modern materials, 11
Morris dancers, 53
moulds, for rushwork, 24, 60

**N**

newspapers, hat blocks, 54
North America, 6, 8, 65
notches, 14
    dog basket, 74–5
    willow letter tray, 92

**O**

oval cane platter, 21–4
oval flower and vegetable
    basket, 82–7

**P**

packing, 14
pairing, 14, 17
pegging, handles, 14, 39
picking off, 14, 17
plaited and stitched baskets, 6
    rush box, 58–63
plastics, 11
pliers, round-nosed, 12
Pollock, Polly, 33
pricking up or down, 14, 18
pulp cane see cane

**R**

rand, 14, 21–2
    English rand, 14, 19
    French rand, 14, 89–93
rapping down, 18
rapping irons, 12
rattan see cane
reed see cane
reverse pairing, 14
reverse waling, 14
ribs, frame baskets, 67–8
rod borders, 14, 25
rods, 14
Roger, Fred, 33
roped handles, 14, 25, 35
round-nosed pliers, 12
rushwork, 10
    boater, 52–7
    box in diagonal weave, 58–63
    checkweave, 56–7, 60
    handling, 15
    moulds, 24, 60
    preparation, 10
    techniques, 24–5

**S**

scalloming, 14, 77, 80
scent, hedgerow materials, 35, 41
scissors, 12
screw blocks, 12
Shakers, 7
shaves, 12
shears, 12
shopping basket, willow, 16–21
side cutters, 12
siding, 15
  rushwork, 24
  willow, 19
sisal rope handles, 83, 86–7
skeining tools, 12
skeins, 15, 78
slath, 15, 17, 21–3
slath rods, 15
slewing, 15, 22, 35, 71, 74
slype, 15, 20
soaking, willow, 9
Somerset, 8
spiralling cane bowl, 46–51

**T**

techniques, 14–25
tips, 15, 17
tools, 12
trac borders, 15, 25, 45
trays: hedgerow materials, 40–5
  willow letter tray, 88–93
twill weave, 15, 59

split slath, 15
square work, 15, 25
  willow letter tray, 88–93
stake and strand baskets, 6, 15, 65
stakes, 15
staking up, 15, 17–18
storage: cane, 9
  rush, 10
  willow, 9
straw, coiled work, 25
strokes, 15
stuff, 15
Swedish lath, 48

**U**

underfoot slath, 15
uprights, 12
upsett, 15
  rushwork, 24
  shopping basket, 18

**V**

vegetable basket, 82–7

**W**

waling, 15, 18, 19
  block, 22–3
  chain, 23
Walpole, Lois, 32
weavers, 15
weights, 12
willow, 7, 8–9
  bolts, 8–9
  brown and white dog basket, 70–5
  dyeing, 11, 83
  fitching, 77, 79–81

frame baskets, 64–9
fruit basket in unstripped willow, 76–81
handling, 15
hedgerow materials, 10–11
letter tray, 88–93
oval flower and vegetable basket, 82–7
preparation, 9
scalloming, 77, 80
shopping basket, 16–21
sizes, 9
skeins, 78
types, 8
working position, 16, 37
woven baskets, 6
Wynter, Sheila, 33, 34–45

**Y**

yarns, 11